AN EXECUTIVE'S GUIDE TO SOFTWARE QUALITY IN AN AGILE ORGANIZATION

A CONTINUOUS IMPROVEMENT JOURNEY

Navid Nader-Rezvani

technologies

CA Press

Apress®

An Executive's Guide to Software Quality in an Agile Organization: A Continuous Improvement Journey

Navid Nader-Rezvani
Los Altos, California, USA

ISBN-13 (pbk): 978-1-4842-3750-2   ISBN-13 (electronic): 978-1-4842-3751-9
https://doi.org/10.1007/978-1-4842-3751-9

Library of Congress Control Number: 2018953013

Managing Director, Apress Media LLC: Welmoed Spahr
Acquisitions Editor: Susan McDermott
Development Editor: Laura Berendson
Coordinating Editor: Rita Fernando

Distributed to the book trade worldwide by Springer Science+Business Media New York, 233 Spring Street, 6th Floor, New York, NY 10013. Phone 1-800-SPRINGER, fax (201) 348-4505, e-mail orders-ny@springer-sbm.com, or visit www.springeronline.com. Apress Media, LLC is a California LLC and the sole member (owner) is Springer Science + Business Media Finance Inc (SSBM Finance Inc). SSBM Finance Inc is a **Delaware** corporation.

For information on translations, please e-mail rights@apress.com, or visit http://www.apress.com/rights-permissions.

Apress titles may be purchased in bulk for academic, corporate, or promotional use. eBook versions and licenses are also available for most titles. For more information, reference our Print and eBook Bulk Sales web page at http://www.apress.com/bulk-sales.

Any source code or other supplementary material referenced by the author in this book is available to readers on GitHub via the book's product page, located at www.apress.com/9781484237502. For more detailed information, please visit http://www.apress.com/source-code.

Printed on acid-free paper

This book is dedicated to the loving memory of my father, Hassan Nader, whose aspirations for me far exceeded my own. His words of encouragement and his faith in my ability have kept me going even a few years after his leaving this world. RIP Dad!

Contents

About the Author

Navid Nader-Rezvani is a passionate executive-engineering leader and an independent consultant with a proven track record as being a change agent, results oriented, and a customer advocate. Navid has successfully led multiple global development and Agile quality organizations and has spent her career breaking down silos, reducing redundant effort, and building collaborative teams. She has a rare set of leadership skills and a unique way of working across organizations and time zones to achieve productivity. Navid has been instrumental in delivering releases on time, on budget, with high-quality outcomes. She has a strong passion for diversity, coaching, mentoring, and volunteering activities and has presented at various conferences. Navid received Bachelor and Master of Science degrees in Electrical Engineering from VA Tech, holds patents, is a certified Scrum Master and SAFe Program Consultant, and is PMP certified.

Find her at https://www.linkedin.com/in/navid-rezvani-9640826.

About the Technical Reviewer

Steve Firestone is the General Manager for Customer Engineering in the Product Organization spanning the entire CA Technologies product portfolio. Some of the initiatives in the CX role include owning product quality and establishing product feedback via telemetry for CA.

Steve was previously the General Manager for the Security Business Unit, where he was heavily engaged in enabling security for cloud, mobile, and SaaS solutions in the diverse and maturing routes to market. Prior to the GM role, Steve led engineering for the Security Business Unit and before that engineering services for security in addition to being a distinguished engineer. Steve has been involved with several corporate strategy initiatives, including big data and analytics. Steve regularly contributes to merger and acquisition activities. Steve has led the center of excellence for Swat/Engineering Services across CA, focused on best practices, knowledge sharing, integration, and innovation opportunities.

Steve has industry experience covering a wide range of technologies and business applications and has teamed with several very large organizations and partners in many different industries. Steve joined CA from a startup and has been known for having a startup mentality within a large company, having done a few, including a very successful zero-to-$2-billion enterprise management solution.

Acknowledgments

I would like to thank my husband and my best friend, Mo Rezvani, whose faith and vote of confidence in my ability to achieve every goal I set for myself has always kept me going. My two sons, Sabah Rezvani and Parsa Rezvani, have also been an incredible source of encouragement and inspiration throughout my career. I wouldn't be where I am today without their love, support, and encouragement. Thank you guys; you mean the world to me!

I would also like to thank the rest of my family, especially my mother, Effat Nader, who taught me to work hard, have faith, and never give up!

In addition, I would like to acknowledge a team of extremely knowledgeable individuals in the field of Agile and Quality Engineering who have spent many hours reviewing various concepts in this book and providing their invaluable feedback. In particular, I would like to thank the following individuals:

- Steve Firestone, whose trust in my ability to engrave quality in the DNA of organizations helped me in multiple stages of my career. He is also the technical reviewer for the book. I am grateful for his focus on this review and fitting it into his extremely busy schedule!

- Dipto Chakravarty, who has always been my strong advocate and a great supporter. His mentorship and ability to focus on my strengths and promote them have taught me a great deal about myself! His subtle references to key quality-impacting areas helped me organize key points and introduce the Five NQPs.

- Rohit Shivram, for his invaluable feedback and thorough review of all chapters.

- Bob Winter, for spending time reviewing details of Agile and perception of quality and providing great feedback based on his own experience in writing his book.

- Sandeep Ramnani, Arun Ramakrishnan, Patty Harasta, Rabeya Akhter, and many other quality-passionate current and former colleagues who have always helped me with quality grassroots initiatives. Their encouragement, willingness to go beyond, and help in reviewing various sections of the book are much appreciated.

- Connie Smallwood and Karen Sleeth, who encouraged me to undertake the book-proposal process.

- Sinead Condon, for delivering a great workshop on Worldview and Integral Map. Her review of the WV and Integral Map chapter and highlighting of how quality integral mapping fits well with the Agile quality journey focus of this book were a great help.

- Various customers at different companies who opened up my view of the world to see that quality is much more than just "defects." Customers' perception of quality led to my holistic approach in looking at quality.

- A writer always needs a good editorial team. Thank you to the editors and publishing advisors: Laura, Rita, and Susan at Apress.

- Last, but not least, I would like to thank all of you for picking up this book and reading through this. I hope that this quality journey resonates with you and you are able to use key concepts in this book to help make quality an integral part of your organization.

I am looking forward to receiving your feedback and hope that, together, we can reshape the perception of quality and realize that it is not someone else's job to own quality!

Preface

You may be wondering why, in creating this book, I have chosen a topic that is known to everyone and considered common sense. Culture of quality is not a new concept, and it is not unique to the software world. The key focus here will be on the mindset transformation and internalization of the culture of quality, which is a bit complex. Engraving it into the DNA of a team, an organization, and the enterprise level will be what is needed to be successful in establishing such a culture.

Throughout my career, I have been fascinated with how placing quality and customers at the center would create happier teams, happier customers, and greater value at a faster pace, as well as generate higher revenue. Demand for software quality is further intensified by the ever-increasing dependence of our world on software.

If you have ever been in a situation where your organization was consumed with attending to a high volume of customer escalations, had challenges with on-time and on-quality releases, or had unhappy and even dysfunctional internal teams and customers, this is the book for you! You will get exposed to practical guidelines from personal experiences on how to reduce the backend of the release, improve the Net Promoter Survey (NPS) scores that enhance revenue, increase customer satisfaction, and reduce the number of customer escalations significantly.

In this book, I share real-life experiences and examples where a focus on holistic quality allowed teams to enjoy significant benefits, such as:

- NPS improvement greater than 200 percent

- Automation coverage improvement greater than 60 percent

- Annual customer escalations reduction by greater than 90 percent

- MTTR (Mean Time to Resolution) reduction by greater than 30 percent

- Productivity enhancement by greater than 85 percent
- Tail end of the release reduction by greater than 50 percent

In many companies, while quality is talked about as being an integral part of the business, it is normally viewed as somebody else's responsibility to own. In the wake of DevTestOps and continuous integration (CI) in the software world, the traditional quality assurance (QA) in a waterfall approach is no longer relevant in many industries. QA's owning quality was often assumed in the waterfall software development lifecycle (SDLC) but is no longer an acceptable argument.

With customers demanding updates faster and focusing more on their experience with new applications and quality of service, the topic of quality is gaining much more attention than ever before. In addition, with the digital transformation and the mobile web application adoption surge, many areas that were not traditionally a big focus, such as the integration of security testing in the development and operations processes (DevSecOps), are gaining a lot of attention in the overall approach to quality.

Today, there are many books out there that focus on the transformation of organizations from waterfall to Agile, with little focus on the role of quality during that transition. There are others that focus only on building an Agile organization, assuming that the culture of quality already exists or will automatically follow. Few focus on Agile testing, DevOps, continuous integration, or fundamentals of scrum, but I have yet to see a book focusing on a holistic quality view. Hence, the drive to write this book. Here, we will drill down into what the holistic quality view is and how it links to overall business enhancements. We will also address challenges associated with the transformation of organizations and provide guidelines on the steps to take to continuously improve all aspects of product quality.

With the introduction of Agile, many organizations have been struggling with how to focus on the overall quality and at the same time deliver value to the customer, introduce new functionalities to the market, and be competitive. Customers look for a swift experience in their digital world, which includes ongoing innovation with quality and predictability. Listening to customers in real time and incorporating their feedback in the solution is the only way to remain competitive.

Quality must be defined and measured for improvements to be achieved. However, the word *quality* lacks a standard definition. Perhaps that is due to the fact that quality is a multidimensional concept. From a customer's point of view, quality is their perceived value of the product they acquire. A customer's satisfaction with the product after they implement a solution is the ultimate validation that the product meets requirements and is fit for use. Even within the customer environment, quality is perceived differently among different internal functions that deal with the vendor (business leaders, sales, admins, technical teams, and their end users).

The holistic view of quality and the five pillars of quality that I have defined in this book can be used as a quality framework and roadmap for teams, organizations, and enterprises to help keep focus on continuous quality process improvement. The real-world examples used in this book allow the reader to learn from such experiences and apply similar strategies and guidelines to help create a quality blueprint for their organization.

The word *transformation* used to have a negative context for many people. It was often a major disruptive event that an organization would go through every couple of years with little positive outcome. Today, business transformation is an integral part of every planning session, and the evolution is more toward continuous business transformation. Having the ability to be faster when responding to challenges as well as establishing the proper mindset required to put a laser focus on quality, make it hard to call it anything but a quality transformation.

In this book, I have captured my personal view along with views from other quality-passionate individuals and include references to personal journeys in transforming various organizations. Such views focus on quality and achieving customer satisfaction and ultimately higher revenue for the enterprise. We will touch upon customer loyalty versus trapped customers, which is a real challenge for many enterprises out there.

Quality is not only about "defects." User experience, quality of service, functionality, and many other factors play into the impression that a product will leave with customers. In many industries even today, the focus is still on cost and new features. In this book, we will focus on best approaches to influence the culture to think as a customer advocate while having the agility that is required in this competitive market.

You may have heard that data is the new currency. With the strong use of social media today, if data show that customers' perception of a vendor is low in regards to the product quality, it will be difficult for that vendor to recover. Addressing this elephant in the room will be key to the success of many organizations and companies as a whole.

In today's competitive world, where more and more people are turning to online purchases for various items, the provided reviews become even more relevant. How many times have you decided to purchase an item online, but then, after seeing legitimate feedback on the item regarding the quality of the product, changed your mind? I personally read all low reviews to understand what customers have said about the perceived quality of the product. If I see too many low reviews, I do not hesitate to move away from that vendor and click on the next.

The same holds true when one downloads a new application from the App Store. If the application doesn't load properly or it is hard to figure out how to log in and get value from it, users not only close the application—they delete it. That is about the extent of the patience today's users have for low quality! Customers today have shorter satisfaction windows and are less willing to wait. They expect vendors to continuously evolve and provide a seamless ability to upgrade and perform.

Building in quality is relevant to any industry and not just the software world. I would like to share a couple of examples (unrelated to the software industry) where thinking "quality first" really brings the message home.

A few years ago, a new general manager joined our company. As a way to get to know his leaders and establish a certain mindset among them, he invited the entire senior leadership team to a workshop, where the main theme was building in quality, collaboration, and putting customers at the center. The workshop got kicked off with a team activity where boxes of unassembled kids' bicycles were made available and teams of two individuals were assigned to assemble each bike. The first three teams to complete the assembly would receive prizes and get recognized. Everyone got to work and took notice of the other teams as they all worked faster to get to the finish line.

Once the allotted time had passed and teams had finished the assembly of their bicycles, a door opened and a few kids (among them a few of the leadership team's kids!) came through. They were told by the general manager they could pick any of the assembled bikes that they liked and go for a ride outside! That is when an interesting thing happened. Almost every team got nervous and quickly picked up their tools to tighten up screws a bit more and check to make sure they were working OK, handles were secured, and the bike was safe to ride!

That example has stuck in my head since that day. While the team was consumed by getting the product to the market fast and ahead of the competition, they had forgotten about their customers' interests and the need to build in quality. Does that sound familiar? I bet some of us have been there and done that!

Another example (unrelated to the software world) of when focusing on customers and building in quality was not an option is the Veresk Bridge construction that served the Trans-Iranian Railway Network before World War II. It was named the Bridge of Victory after World War II due to its significant strategic location during the war and is registered on the National Heritage List. It is considered one of the masterpieces of world architecture. The king of Persia had hired foreign engineers to help build a magnificent bridge with cement, bricks, and sand (no metal.) The project got completed in 1937 (see Figure I-1).

Figure I-1. Veresk Bridge[1]

During the bridge's inauguration, the king himself attended the ceremony. It was said that he first thanked the lead engineer, his entire crew, and their families for their magnificent work. However, since there were concerns from people that the narrow bridge might not be strong enough to support the weight of the train, the king asked the lead engineer and his family to stand under the bridge while the first train passed over. After all, he did not use any rebar in the concrete, and concrete has no resistance to tension; a whole new design concept! The monumental bridge is now over 80 years old and still serves the passengers!

---

[1]Thanks to Mohammad Razavi for taking the photo and Nariman Nader for coordinating it.

The preceding examples leave no room to question the importance of building in quality, considering the user experience, and dealing with customers' perception of quality. Being able to deliver a product that meets customers' requirements, is easy to use, and is competitive requires a unique quality mindset. Guiding an organization on how to keep the critical balance of delivering new features and value to customers while attending to continuous quality improvement remains challenging. This requires a full understanding of quality, including what it means to the product teams and how it is perceived by customers. Often, those two don't coincide!

Introduction

Imagine a world where product quality is integrated into every function in your organization. Developers, quality engineers, product managers, leaders at all levels, sales, services, and support work together and focus on a shared vision. That vision consists of delivering quality value to customers and enabling a fast flow of planned work into production. I know that may be a bit of a stretch of the imagination for most organizations, but the path and guidance on how to get there over time is what we will be focusing on here.

Every time we ask our customers about our product quality, they focus on their total experience in dealing with our product and teams. Their quality perception starts from the moment they search for a solution online and keeps going as they deal with our sales team, internal product team, and support organization throughout the usage of the solution. In other words, they value their entire user journey with their vendor.

Many organizations have adopted Agile as a practice to deliver high-quality product releases with high value to the market faster. While it is crucial to focus on the mechanics of Agile disciplines internally, it is also important to define what quality is, how customers view quality, and how it actually impacts customer satisfaction and loyalty in such a way that it brings additional business opportunities and enhances revenue. Many teams have historically focused on product releases that are rich in new features while giving little attention to improving the customer experience on existing features. Lack of focus on continuous improvement along with not engaging end users to gather feedback have created friction and in many cases have cost companies revenue due to losing customer loyalty.

In today's digital world, there is no shortage of data. Collecting relevant data, analyzing it, and using telemetry can play a big role in the quality journey when delivering relevant solutions to customers and improving upon them at all times. With telemetry we can pivot and redirect our focus to adapt our ways of doing business to deliver the best value to our customers. Yet, telemetry is not fully adopted in most companies with legacy code and features.

Having data articulated in the form of ROI (Return on Investment) to explain to the business and executive leadership team the importance of investing in a quality-improvement journey leaves little room for debate. Giving quality-related initiatives a high priority for investment should be an integral part of delivering software. And throughout, we must remember that improving quality is a journey and not a destination—an idea that is vital to any organization's quality transformation success.

How to Use This book

This book is written in such a way that each chapter can be read independently and still offer key messages for interested individuals. Of course, it is best to follow the flow and read from the beginning to the end.

The book is divided into various chapters, each focusing on a unique aspect of quality. It also covers topics and examples around Agile disciplines and the transformation of organizations from waterfall to Agile. There is also a reference to the Integral Theory and Worldview that provides visibility into how human beings look at providing solutions to the problems they are faced with.

After the initial read, each chapter could be used as an independent reference if and when the reader is in need of a refresher on the topic. The NQPs (Navid's Quality Pillars) that I have laid out in this book can be used for any industry, and once internalized they can serve as a great set of tools to continuously improve upon and measure key quality-impacting factors.

If you are new to Agile and are going through a transition at this point, I would highly encourage you to read Chapter 1 and the examples listed in Chapter 4. Then, you can focus on other chapters, particularly on Chapter 5, to get familiar with the Five Pillars of Quality and understand what quality is and how it can be woven into the culture so that teams seek to continuously improve.

The examples used in this book start with quality improvements at the product-team level then extend to the business unit with multiple product lines. The last segment of this book is focused on quality at scale. This is where you will find a set of guidelines based on personal experience regarding how to get the entire enterprise aligned and transformed into the culture of Agile quality.

Real-world examples listed in this book will provide practical guidelines for every team to follow. Every team is at a different maturity level, so when you read through the pillars of quality, keep challenges related to your organization in mind. Create a set of notes on what issue is high in priority in terms of the value to the customers, happier internal teams, and its impact on the overall revenue.

If you have like-minded people at work, it is best to do a group study and discuss various topics. The interpretation of topics related to Agile and quality vary from one function to another. In any organizational transformation, unless there is a social contract with the team members, executive leadership team, and all levels of management for their support, you will find it difficult to go through significant changes. So, I highly encourage you to invite your leaders to such discussions. Looking at problems through different lenses will be a great stepping stone in your journey. Playing into the motivational level for team members and leadership at all levels will also be critical.

Once teams have acknowledged the need for change, internalized the common objectives, and can articulate the challenges and the need to do things differently, you can consider a significant milestone in your journey to have been achieved. This is the reason for touching upon concepts such as the Quality Integral Map and Worldview later in this book.

A book-club approach or meetup within your organization at all levels to define problems and map examples in this book to possible situations in your organization will be another great approach to follow. Understanding the overall value stream, double-clicking (going deeper) on the steps and areas that are impacting productivity, and articulating other problems you need to find solutions for will be a great place to start this journey.

A couple of sections were reviewed by other quality- and Agile-passionate individuals and capture their specific views as well. Please remember that not everyone agrees 100 percent with the selected approaches. Also, the same methodologies used in one company may need adjustments to be effective in another due to their cultural differences, the nature of their business, and other circumstances. So, please keep that in mind when you go through various examples in this book and are trying to map them against your own company's list of challenges.

At the end of each chapter, there are questions that will promote group and team discussions to help map what is described in each chapter with your specific working environment. There are a few universities that have software design quality as part of their curriculum today. This book can be used as a reference to link the theoretical learnings with real-world practices.

I hope you enjoy reading this book as much as I enjoyed writing it! Happy Reading!

Quality in Agile

How the Two Fit Together

I don't want to sound like Agile is the answer to all our problems in releasing software with high quality. After all, for many years companies had released software, sent human beings to the moon, built aircraft, and achieved many more accomplishments via a waterfall software development lifecycle (SDLC) process. However, with the fast evolution of technology, we have no choice but to adopt Agile and deliver high-quality, incremental value faster.

Taking a moment to understand what problem Agile really solves will help navigate and ground leaders who may think Agile is the silver bullet to resolve their quality problems. A lot of people who are first introduced to Agile think that it helps them deliver product to market faster. That is actually not the objective of Agile! In fact, one can argue that Agile will slow down the ultimate time to market and introduce overhead that is certainly well worth the gain. But this is not what most people expect.

Agile allows for the delivery of an accurate solution to the market. Keep in mind that engaging customers along the way will enable teams to react and adapt to the needs of those customers. With more iterations, you have the opportunity to put smaller pieces of functionality out in the market and thus receive feedback more quickly. However, delivering a full solution compared to the old SDLC process could be slower. I think you will all agree that while speed is important, there is no point to being fast in delivering a useless solution to customers!

© CA 2019
N. Nader-Rezvani, *An Executive's Guide to Software Quality in an Agile Organization*,
https://doi.org/10.1007/978-1-4842-3751-9_1

The focus of this book is mostly on the transformation and quality-improvement journey that has dependencies on the culture of the organization, the technology that they deliver, and their customers' appetite for the right level of agility. Culture does not change overnight. It is a reflection of the employees and the company as a whole. Leaders should enable teams and create an environment for the culture to grow. Inclusivity and consistency will be very important in transforming the culture. Everyone in the organization should be involved in continuous evolution and transformation, especially the people who are closer to the customers.

Pure Agile may only exist in an academic world. In the real world, it is all about continuous motion and transformation to help influence many years of legacy practices and ways of thinking around quality and customer expectations. Adopting practices that will allow organizations to continuously deliver value to customers should be considered a key priority when organizations decide to embark on this quality journey. Initially, such practices may not align exactly with the mature Agile practices. But, over time, the team will evolve and get better.

As an example, Agile purists may not support hardening sprints or separate level 2 sustaining teams. They may even cringe when they learn about organizations that have set aside planned time for hardening or have a separate level 2 sustaining team. The reality is that, unless you have experienced Agile teams, full automation, no legacy code, and no certification requirements, you may need hardening and level 2 sustaining support. Organizations just starting Agile will need more time to focus on key areas such as automation that will help them improve their processes over time. I always advise teams to be patient with themselves while embarking on their Agile quality journey and learn how to crawl before they walk.

The biggest benefit of using Agile is to deliver value to customers faster. Breaking complex problems into smaller pieces is one powerful technique that will help in doing so. This process needs to be fully adopted and accepted at all levels of the organization for it to be effective. If the leaders are skeptical about the value Agile brings to their organization and are not true believers, it is almost guaranteed that the product teams will not be successful. In the Agile quality transformation, the leaders' commitment to quality and continuous improvement is critical and cannot be delegated. After all, as "they" say, a change will go no further than the mindset of the leaders who lead it.

Another challenge in implementing Agile is when one function in the company has adopted Agile, but the rest are still functioning in a waterfall manner. For example, if the engineering teams have made the shift, but sales, education, and support haven't bought into the Agile practices, friction develops, which will lead to failure in delivering value to the customers.

A key principle in Agile is working as a team. Agile is a team sport, and collaboration is not negotiable. A few years ago, my boys attended Michael Jordan's basketball camp. One of the enduring lessons they learned is the importance of collaboration and teamwork. They learned that while talent alone may win a game, teamwork and intelligence are key to winning a championship!

Why am I talking about Agile when the focus of this book is product quality? Although quality is all about building things right, understanding *how* to build the right thing has a significant influence on the customers' perception of quality. Also, quality is a foundational element in Agile. Leveraging various frameworks that will lead organizations through this important and difficult journey will allow companies to stay competitive and operate in a constantly changing world.

Building the right thing can be made easier when you have a strong culture of quality and an Agile mindset, as well as a process framework that leads to delivering incremental value. I have been brought into multiple organizations to address their quality challenges when the first dilemma for the executive team is why their product quality still suffers after "going Agile." By "going Agile" they usually mean investing time and money in delivering Agile training and adopting Agile ceremonies. They sometimes overlook the need for executives to focus on creating an environment where teams can thrive. This is where I usually start, diving deeper into their Agile implementation and focusing on Quality Integral Mapping, which I will cover in the next chapter, to help analyze such situations.

The most important part of Agile is to work iteratively by collaborating and achieving incremental value. Many organizations that call themselves Agile, focus more on the Agile ceremonies and assume that by following such processes they are automatically ready to deliver software faster and with higher quality. Often the required tools and framework—and, most important, the right quality mindset—are ignored. Usually that is because the investment required for developing people, processes, and tooling does not get considered as part of the overall strategy.

Agile Principles and Myths

Every organization that associates itself with the Agile world explains its journey and transformation in a different way. With few exceptions, they all complain about implementation challenges. There is a lot to be learned when you go deeper into their understanding of the Agile principles and the way they are stated in the Agile Manifesto (agilemanifesto.org):

MANIFESTO FOR AGILE SOFTWARE DEVELOPMENT

We are uncovering better ways of developing software by doing it and helping others do it. Through this work we have come to value:

- Individuals and interactions over processes and tools

- Working software over comprehensive documentation

- Customer collaboration over contract negotiation

- Responding to change over following a plan

That is, while there is value in the items on the right, we value the items on the left more.

Kent Beck	James Grenning	Robert C. Martin
Mike Beedle	Jim Highsmith	Steve Mellor
Arie van Bennekum	Andrew Hunt	Ken Schwaber
Alistair Cockburn	Ron Jeffries	Jeff Sutherland
Ward Cunningham	Jon Kern	Dave Thomas
Martin Fowler	Brian Marick	

© 2001, the above authors

This declaration may be freely copied in any form, but only in its entirety through this notice.

I am sure some of you have come across the following comments/myths:

- We are Agile, therefore we don't have much time to waste on writing down our test cases!

- We provide no documentation as we focus more on getting working software quickly with no time to waste on documenting something that could go obsolete as we change the functionality!

- It is the responsibility of our product management team to interact with customers and tell us what to build. We deliver what product management asks for and try not to slow things down by over analyzing different approaches to delivering on time!

- Our direction keeps changing as new priorities show up in our backlog. As a result, Agile will not be a good fit for us, as we wouldn't be able to release a complete solution ever!

- We believe that Agile is only effective for small projects. When it comes to our large projects, we still follow our Agile team model, but we need a specific project plan to ensure clear coordination and integration with larger teams while keeping our scope untouched!

You may believe that your organization is not in such dire need of learning the details of Agile principles. However, since your focus is on improving product quality, diving deeper into Agile principles and being aware of how certain Agile implementations may actually hurt your product quality is important.

Having transparency and ensuring information moves up and down an organization are the key cultural changes that are needed in any transformation. Evolving continuously and acknowledging that the new world is all about continuous motion and not a fixed state will allow organizations to be prepared to respond to change with minimal disruption to their normal delivery plans. It is not possible to hold off on all initiatives and new functionalities and only focus on the Agile quality transformation. It needs to be integrated in the vision for the organization. Committing to excellence and continuous improvement will be the key to success in the long journey of continuous quality improvement.

Basic Agile Concepts

We often forget that built-in quality is expected as one of the foundational elements of Agile principles. That is the reason why I am going to go into a bit more detail around Agile transformation and delivery—quality is "table stakes" in the world of Agile. If implemented properly, Agile ensures that in every iteration, quality standards are reflected and built in. Quality is not an afterthought and can't be bolted on later. Built-in quality is a prerequisite for going Agile and is not optional. Customers expect solutions that work and are often more forgiving on a slight date change if it means a higher-quality solution for them.

The move from traditional to Agile methods is not always straightforward. Almost every organization needs assistance to achieve such transitions and improve their Agile capabilities. Several frameworks have been developed to guide organizations in Agile process improvement and Agile adoption. Here are just a few examples of such frameworks:

- Agile Software Solution Framework (ASSF[1]) provides an overall context for exploring various Agile methods and includes an Agile Toolkit for quantifying different parts of Agile.

---

[1]https://pdfs.semanticscholar.org/818e/e2da90a2284f86e2719b51c5a25 debf147be.pdf

- Scaled Agile Framework (SAFe[2]) can help with creating an Agile organizational structure at the portfolio, program, and team levels.

- Lean Agile (LA[3]) is a marriage between Agile development and lean practices. The focus is on key principles around eliminating waste and continuous process improvement (see Kaizen below), respecting people, building in quality, delivering quickly, and optimizing the whole.

■ **Kaizen (or Continuous Improvement)** This is a long-term approach to achieving small, incremental improvements in processes to improve efficiency and quality. Kaizen has been used in lean manufacturing for a long time. If Kaizen is adopted, continuous process improvement (CPI) is the responsibility of the entire organization and not just a selected few. This concept has been mapped to the software development industry, and many Agile frameworks follow major principles of Kaizen.

Key Terminology

Here is some terminology related to Agile implementation that is referenced in this book:

Scrum: An iterative Agile development framework for developing products.

Iteration/Sprint: A predefined work period within which product is produced. The duration usually varies between two and four weeks.

Scrum Team: A scrum team consists of a cross-functional group of people who perform the work. They self-organize, estimate the work, commit to it, and deliver against their commitment. Functions that are associated with each scrum team are development, quality engineering, technical documentation, product owner (PO), and scrum master (SM). They, of course, have direct access to the architect for the product.

Product Owner (PO): PO is the liaison between the scrum team and external customers, as well as among internal functions, such as management, finance, sales, and support.

Scrum Master (SM): SM is a servant leader for the scrum team. SM coordinates and facilitates all team events and works on fielding impediments that slow the team down. SM is the keeper of the scrum process.

---

[2]https://www.youtube.com/watch?v=tmJ_mJw8xec
[3]https://www.youtube.com/watch?v=_I15bPa5_Gw

DoR and DoD: Definition of Ready (DoR) is critical to ensure success for Agile teams. As part of regular refinement, teams will continue to refine stories, and once they are clear on the objectives and acceptance criteria, they can mark them as "ready." That will speed up the implementation phase once teams start their iteration.

Some teams confuse Definition of Done (DoD) and acceptance criteria. DoD applies to all stories, but every story has its own unique acceptance criteria.

Many teams miss the backlog grooming, DoR, and a clear DoD and wonder why their Agile implementation is not that effective!

Backlog Refinement (Grooming)

The flow of work in Agile can be a bit confusing at first. Prioritization and backlog refinement are led by the PO, while input is provided by the scrum team members on an ongoing basis. Regular grooming of the backlog will allow the team to collaborate, ask clarifying questions, and estimate the effort required for the stories. Such backlog grooming sessions are held at least once per sprint—or preferably once a week. This effort allows for the team backlog to have stories that are ready for implementation with minimal risk and surprise.

Sprint (Iteration) Planning

Once stories are groomed, the sprint planning can be expected to go smoothly. The sprint planning session takes anywhere from two to four hours and is facilitated by a scrum master. The main purpose of this planning meeting is to clarify objectives and priorities and ensure all objectives are feasible. It is also important to have captured feedback from prior iteration(s) so as to discuss key points that need to be addressed in the upcoming sprints. The team will then pick a small number of items from the list to improve on and include on the sprint backlog as they see fit. If the prioritized list of improvements is not agreed upon by the scrum team and written down, it is not guaranteed to get done!

Daily Standup

During the sprint, team members work hard to deliver against their commitment. Daily standup meetings (no more than 15 to 20 minutes) are when team members communicate with one another about what they worked on, what is remaining to be done, and bring up any blocking issues that need attention. Scrum master and team members keep an eye on the progress and remaining work to ensure successful completion of the sprint.

End of Sprint Demo

On the last day of the sprint, the team conducts a demo to showcase the great work that they accomplished. This provides visibility on the work that was done and allows for major feedback to be considered for upcoming sprints.

Sprint Retrospective

After the demo, a retrospective session is conducted to focus on desired improvements. This meeting is for the members of the scrum, including the PO and SM. Teams consider the progress and roadblocks they had during the sprint and come up with recommendations to follow for future sprints to work more effectively as a team. SM is a key contributor in the retrospective meetings and will follow up on any impediments and any areas that will need help from the broader organization.

Here are three major areas that get discussed in a retrospective session:

- What went well?
- What did not go well?
- What changes does the team want to make for the next sprint?

Prioritizing the Backlog for Better Workflow

Most Agile teams develop on cadence and release on demand. This shows that despite some beliefs, Agile teams care about dates and meet their commitments. Business owners need to understand how prioritization works in Agile and how it is important to fix quality but not scope.

Customer Engagement

If Agile is presented and implemented well, customers will see it as an opportunity to influence the way software is built. They will also get access to working software more frequently, with an opportunity to provide immediate feedback on functionality and usability. Incorporating such early feedback into future designs and eliminating the frustrations that surface with fixed-date and fixed-scope approaches is a big change from how the traditional waterfall approach worked. That was when customers would see a complete implementation of a feature close to when the software was scheduled to go GA (General Availability), giving customers little opportunity to provide feedback.

Vision and Quality Objectives

Understanding the vision, roadmap, and quality objectives for a release, as well as iteration goals, will provide clarity on what is expected of the scrum teams. It will also provide visibility on what stakeholders, who are focused on the overall business, should expect at various stages of the release. This alignment will result in higher engagement, better value delivery, higher internal productivity and collaboration, and higher customer satisfaction.

Built-in quality is a given in the world of Agile. You can't move fast if you don't have a good understanding of quality objectives. Transparency builds trust and goes hand in hand with accountability. Transparency, trust, and a clear understanding of quality objectives are all key to an organization's ability to work effectively together.

The Importance of Innovation

Let us not forget about the role of innovation in Agile. It is important to highlight that innovation is about new value and not necessarily new things! This is a key concept, as most people don't view process innovation as being as important as feature innovation is.

We hear over and over that investing in innovation programs pays off significantly. Steve Healey (head of new ideas at BT Telecom) had mentioned during an interview[4] that for every $1 invested in their innovation program, they returned over $75 to the business. That is significant!

Because there is always pressure and intense focus on customer-value delivery, it is hard to set time aside to innovate. Some enterprises set aside an Innovation and Planning iteration for research or "FedEx days"/hackathons. Giving teams time to recharge their batteries and work on whatever they are interested in, as long as it reflects the mission of the company, can boost morale and leads to better engagement by team members. Perhaps we should introduce the ROI of giving employees an opportunity to have fun and work on something that they are passionate about from time to time. The learnings from such events can make their way into the backlog and help drive innovation.

Process innovation often gets ignored, but it needs to be considered, as it impacts internal productivity, ability to achieve higher product quality, and delivery of higher value to customers. Teams that have integrated the culture of process innovation into their release cadence have reported higher program execution efficiency, release predictability, happier internal team members, and happier customers!

---

[4]http://www.futurenautics.com/2016/05/slide-show/
http://www.brightidea.com/resources/steve-healey-measuring-the-business-impact-of-innovation/

Figure 1-1 shows a handy framework that can be used for process innovation.

Vision: Quality is engraved in the mindset of all employees and is demonstrated daily in everything we do

Strategy: Continuous process improvement initiatives and programs that are focused on improving quality and customer experience

Tactics: Cross-Functional Quality Improvements; Develop Culture of Quality; Leadership Accountability

Process Innovation: Define quality problems from customer perspective; define key metrics and measure against, communicate best practices and encourage continuous improvement mindset; reward appropriate behaviors

Figure 1-1. Role of process innovation in a quality focused organization

Leadership Challenges in an Agile Quality Transformation

In order for a transformation to work, leadership must take ownership of the results. This includes a personal commitment to higher quality and continuous improvement. The right culture will not emerge if leaders are not on board. You may have heard about having a social contract between executives and team members when the culture is to be changed. What this means is that the executive team voices a commitment to supporting the transformation and to acting as a servant leader to help guide and support teams through the difficult journey.

Many executives want to implement Agile because they have heard that it will enable them to deliver faster, but they don't bother to understand what their role is in this initiative or fully internalize that adopting Agile methodologies may not necessarily mean delivering a full solution faster. Delivering incremental value to your customers is how Agile can help teams. So, when teams adopt Agile and consider proper steps to build in quality, often providing time estimates for incremental delivery that are not aligned with what leaders had in mind, conflicts and tension may arise. This leads to an unhealthy working environment and is a recipe for confusion and frustration in the organization.

To implement any change, the leadership team needs to focus on the "why," especially if the change involves the entire organization at all levels. Once they internalize why it is important to make the shift and are willing to have a social contract with their teams, it removes unnecessary emotions and allows for all functions to align and deliver against a common vision. The issue in many cases is that we jump right into the how and what and try to implement new processes without knowing why!

Here are some key characteristics of successful transformational leaders:

- Communicate clearly with all levels of their organization to ensure the rationale for change is understood

- Always present and don't hide in their offices

- Show their commitment by example and by changing how they behave

- Continuously reinforce change and take the time to listen to concerns

- Open to constructive feedback

- Live and believe in the cause

I was once hired by a company that had just started its Agile transformation journey for its entire enterprise. The first thing I noticed was that there was a disconnect between the transformation project sponsor and the executive team, including the CEO of the company.

Teams spent many long hours prioritizing the items that they needed to work on to allow them to deliver on a set cadence and in parallel to ensure time was dedicated to reducing technical debt and improving product quality. Once the executive management team learned that the release dates were getting impacted as a result of the new process, they started to micro manage the team and made it difficult for them to focus on their initiative.

Needless to say, that transformation, despite the effort and cost to the company, came to a halt. This was the result of the CEO and his staff's desiring to go Agile without their internalizing the required investment and impact. It was initially agreed to because it was being talked about by the competition, sounded cool, and was expected to resonate well with the customers. In their mind, Agile was some sort of fancy model to gain attention from their customers; they did not really understand their own role in making it happen.

Many concepts in Agile may seem easy to understand but can be challenging to fully internalize and master. Implementing and adopting some processes is relatively simple, but they will fail to have an impact if the Agile mindset does not come with it. A commitment to creating an environment where people can freely share their ideas, be transparent, hold each other accountable, and have a healthy debate is difficult to establish. Transparency, innovation, collaboration, and keeping customers at the center when key product decisions are made will help product teams better understand the "why" and the vision. That will allow teams to focus on delivering value to customers.

Change is always difficult, and at times unsettling. Most executives look for a silver bullet to transform their organization and expect to realize their quality-improvement objectives overnight. Agile transformation is a journey and requires a culture of learning, transparency, and accountability. Understanding that human beings won't internalize change unless they see value at a personal level is also important. While adoption at the grassroots levels will be key for any change to sustain, it is critical to ensure there is also accountability and willingness to change at the executive leadership level. One without the other will lead to an unsuccessful transformation.

Creating a culture of planning, execution, innovation, and delivering feedback and retrospectives in all functions and levels of the organization with full transparency will lead to a successful and collaborative team. Let us also not forget about the value of having an experienced coach with your team throughout this journey. If your organization doesn't have one, I highly recommend investing there!

It is crucial for the executive leaders of the company to be in regular communication across various levels of the organization. Explaining why the company is changing their product-development practices and what it will mean for the entire company is important in any transformation. Adopting a common vocabulary and meaningful metrics will help organizations focus on the outcome and values and be more supportive of the required changes.

Once critical objectives are identified, internalized, and clearly articulated at the executive level, a cross-functional group of leaders needs to drive the initiative and be held accountable for the transformation of the organization. This team establishes regular communication with their respective organization on detailed goals, milestones, plans, what success looks like, expected outcomes, and next steps. They are also responsible for understanding the organizational challenges, removing obstacles, and updating the executive team on the adoption of such changes. Over communication at all levels of the organization about the initiative is key for success. We will dive deeper into this topic when we discuss quality transformation at scale in a later chapter.

Any adjustment to the plan is to be discussed, and feedback must be captured and implemented accordingly. Once the goals are understood and benefits are articulated at all levels of the organization, the transformation team will help in operationalizing changes, managing the adoption, routing escalations, listening to feedback, providing training and coaching, and doing appropriate tooling, all to take the organization to the next level.

In the upcoming sections, we will cover specific examples and steps that have been used to help an organization successfully transform by influencing the culture, providing a clear vision, and establishing the mindset to focus on delivering value. This requires leadership that leads by example, takes responsibility for failure, and understands that going down this path is a journey and not a fixed destination.

It is important to highlight that Agile must be scaled at all levels before the overall value is observed. In the world of Agile there is no more command and control. Leadership is no longer the domain of only leaders or an organizational layer that alone can make decisions. Their role remains critical in setting the strategy, providing guidance along the journey, and then getting out of the way for teams to execute, implement, and make appropriate decisions.

In order to gain business agility, the decision-making process needs to be streamlined, or else minimizing the time to solution is not possible. Every team member is accountable for decisions and must demonstrate the ability to lead. Leaders need to create an environment that empowers individuals and teams to lead. A reminder that all focus should be on finding the best solutions for customers will allow those closest to the work to make the best choices. Having the ability to change and pivot as an organization with little resistance will be key to staying competitive. This is often the hardest mindset change for leaders and organizations as a whole.

Knowledge is no longer power! It is, however, the catalyst for delivering value if it is gained through experience and engagement. This is another cultural change that needs to be emphasized. Keeping knowledge and information in silos will promote heroism and will prevent organizations from leveraging, learning, and delivering the best solutions to customers. Establishing a reward system to encourage collaboration and accountability is important in any type of transformation.

As mentioned earlier, a strong commitment (in the form of a social contract) is required to have a successful quality transformation. Having a leadership team trained in both lean thinking and the adoption of key Agile principles for on-going decision-making processes and continuous quality improvement should be one of the initial phases of this initiative.

With a social contract comes responsibility for internalizing Agile principles, leading by example, listening to concerns, removing roadblocks, supporting required investments in people and processes, and enabling teams to obtain the necessary tools to practice and train others. This contract is not just limited to the leaders; the entire team also agrees on what is expected of them. They agree to respect others, collaborate, and strengthen their individual working relationship with their team in a self-organized environment.

Every time teams find themselves at a decision point where there is a need for greater leadership support, they know exactly where to go and who to talk to. Without such a social contract, organizations would be dealing with grassroots efforts that might not sustain the transformation long term (similar to the failed transformation that I mentioned earlier). Leaders are expected to be present and to truly believe in investing in people to build a stronger team. We all know that happy and informed teams will develop and deliver solutions that satisfy customers.

One of the most critical things to keep in mind when using Agile methodologies to develop software is to manage your queue and reduce the work in progress (WIP). Often, a leader comes in with a new request that was promised to a customer after the teams have already discussed their backlog and are well on their way to executing against their planned iteration/release. When they ask if this new work has higher priority than what the team had planned to do, the answer is unclear. There is an unspoken expectation to do this new request on top of everything else that is planned. This is where a decisive business owner is needed; they must rearrange priorities and remove ambiguity around what to deliver next. It is critical for leaders to understand Agile principles and how a backlog is created and prioritized.

Remember, it is not sufficient just to "do Agile." Creating an Agile quality mindset, thinking Agile, and being Agile need to be the focus. Establishing the best and most relevant organizational alignment, understanding best approaches to measuring success, and promoting a culture of transparency and trust are key elements of a successful transformation journey. We will next focus on proper metrics to help you measure and continuously improve.

Key Agile Metrics

We cannot improve on what is not measured! Without data and measurements, improvement and maturity are hard to achieve. In software engineering, this area still needs a lot of focus. Metrics should be well thought through before being put in use. I have seen many examples where selected metrics have actually been harmful to the quality transformation of an organization.

In one organization, a metric was used to measure standup frequency by teams. Even though most of the team members didn't feel like their standups were effective or that they were getting any benefits from attending, just to fulfill that metric, they would get together every day. Conversations would sometimes go on for hours, and some individuals would lose interest and start playing with their phones or answering emails. But, at least they were showing up on some corporate score card as a team that was doing Agile and holding regular standups!

In another organization, having zero defects was chosen as a metric for all teams to comply with. While the intent was commendable, we learned that some teams stopped testing toward the end of the release out of fear of finding defects late in the game. Or they kept track of their defects in a spreadsheet separate from their main defect tracking system. They all passed the objective by showing zero defects as a metric that they were being assessed upon. However, bad behavior was being promoted and quality was being compromised.

Understanding what to measure and what outcome you are looking for will help in determining what metrics to use at what stage of Agile quality maturity. Concrete metrics will allow for timely conversations and will provide tangible data for continuous improvement and retrospective discussions. For example, if your focus initially is to achieve higher productivity, you can start with the following metrics:

- Completing actual vs. planned number of stories/points (including technical debt planned stories)
- Broken build frequency
- Code coverage
- Mean Time to Repair/Resolution (MTTR)

Lead time and cycle time used to be the popular metrics to help with increasing velocity in various sections of the code-delivery process. A key metric that will help with being predictable with customers is measuring the flow time. This encompasses the total time it takes from the first customer request through to completion. Over time, that type of data can help organizations quantify the probability of completing a certain percentage of work in a defined cadence. After all, achieving the greatest customer value requires consistent delivery of the best solutions.

Key areas that Agile can be effective in are:

- Achieving a better release predictability and building in quality
- Achieving a higher level of productivity
- Obtaining valuable and timely feedback from customers on the provided values
- Elevating customer satisfaction
- NPS (Net Promoter Survey) score reflecting higher product quality
- Attracting and retaining happier employees

Choosing metrics that relate to the preceding areas, depending on where the team is in their transformation journey and their maturity, can be an effective way to ensure continuous quality improvement in an Agile world.

I have seen organizations where a large number of metrics are identified, but focusing on all of them is almost impossible. After a while, teams stop reporting against them, especially if data is gathered manually and is not easily obtainable. Metrics will provide visibility into the current state. Reviewing such data, identifying key areas to improve on, and translating that data into actionable tasks will help keep the focus on improving quality.

This is another area where having trained and experienced Agile coaches will facilitate conversations and help the teams pick the most relevant metrics. Ensuring that Agile coaches are high enough in the organization to influence such metrics and help guide not only the scrum teams but also the executive team members will be an effective way to maneuver through change.

Leading and Lagging Indicators

Metrics can be categorized into two different sections:

- Leading indicators – Speak to the data that provides visibility into the quality of software even before it is released

- Lagging indicators – Relate to the data that is available after the software is shipped

As maturity is achieved in organizations, monitoring leading and lagging indicators will allow teams to consider the factors with the highest impact on quality, perform root-cause and volume-driver analyses, and create stories to address such items as part of the continuous quality improvement journey.

Tables 1-1 and 1-2 show some examples of leading and lagging indicators that some teams have used successfully to track their quality improvements. It is important to choose leading and lagging indicators that are meaningful based on the maturity of the organization. As teams get more experienced and the culture of quality is established, additional metrics can be considered and monitored.

Table 1-1. Examples of Leading Indicators

Metric	Operational Definition	Formula
% Code Coverage (Unit Test & Functional)	% of code covered by automated QA testing/unit testing/integration testing.	(number of lines of code exercised) / (total number of lines of code)*100
% Tests Automated (Unit Test & Functional)	% tests automated for the release.	(number of tests automated / total number of automatable tests for the release)*100
% Story Completion Rate	Story completion rate in given release. The ability to plan and complete the story (meeting the "done" criteria).	number of story points completed / number of story points planned
MTTR (INT) --- Defect Trend	The number of defects resolved in a month/week.	Σ(created date-resolved date)/# of defects.
% of Pass to Plan and Run to Plan Tests	% of test case execution and coverage	number of passed test cases / total number of test cases identified by Scrum team to provide good coverage for features
Build Time	Key index for continuous integration.	amount of time that is required to validate the health of check ins

Table 1-2. Examples of Lagging Indicators

Metric	Operational Definition	Formula
% of Hot Fixes	Number of emergency fixes provided to the customer.	calculated quarterly
CES	Number of customer escalated issues in a predefined interval.	total number CES per product line % of CES resolution as per provided ETA
MTTR (EXT)	The number of defects resolved in a month/week will give MTTR for that particular month/week.(Post development Cycle)	Σ(created date-resolved date) / number of defects.
Product Health Score Card	A letter grade that is assigned to the quality of releases as per pre-defined set of metrics; i.e., TCO (upgradability, usability, supportability, MTTR, any other customer specific metrics.	average of scores for each of the agreed upon metrics
DCE by Release	The amount of defects which your process detects as a proportion of all defects (those which you do and do not detect).	number of defects found internally during the release / (number of defects found internally during the iteration + number of defects found by customers for the release)

Teams should remember that the same metrics that promote a culture of quality and continuous improvement for on-premises products may be different than what needs to be considered for SaaS (Software as a Service).

For example, in addition to the mentioned metrics, some key metrics that are more relevant to an SaaS environment are:

- Mean time to identify root cause – Refers to ability to debug the code

- Mean time to identify a fix – Reflects the expertise/level of training needed/code complexity

- Mean time to deploy

- Availability & unplanned downtime (i.e., 5 9's)[5]

The key takeaway is to educate team members and leaders that the objective is not only to have a green scorecard against selected metrics. These metrics are there to prompt conversations and good behaviors and help create a culture of quality where continuous improvement is engraved into the DNA of the entire organization!

---

[5]Downtime in a production environment is measured based on the number of 9s. For example, 5 9's (99.999% of time of uptime) means unplanned downtime due to various issues is less than 5.25 minutes per year.

Self-Reflection Questions

- What barriers to continuous transformation exist in your organization?
- What is the main objective of implementing Agile in an organization?
- Why is having a social contract at all levels important?
- What are key characteristics of a transformational leader?
- What are some key metrics that are relevant while a team is going through their quality transformation journey?
- What is SAFe?
- What are some myths about the effectiveness of Agile?
- How should standups get conducted?
- How should a leader get his or her organization on board with the objectives of new initiatives?
- What are some key metrics for teams that start their quality journey?
- What are examples of leading and lagging indicators for your company?
- What are examples of some metrics that could promote bad behaviors in teams?

Worldview and Integral Map

Looking at Problems Through Different Lenses

Before I walk you through specific examples where quality challenges were addressed by a team and organization, it is important to draw your attention to a concept to which I was introduced by one of my colleagues: Worldview (WV) and Integral Mapping. As a human being, the experiences we have are by-products of our WV—how we see problems and how we deal with them. In this section, I will walk you through the concept and how it is important to talk about these critical and proven factors in your organization before expecting a unified result and DNA-changing actions.

Worldview (WV)

I participated in a workshop, facilitated by a colleague, in which she unpacked the term *worldview* and associated it with practical application. We first reviewed the definition of *worldview*:

Merriam-Webster Dictionary[1]:

A comprehensive conception or apprehension of the world especially from a specific standpoint

---

[1]https://www.merriam-webster.com/dictionary/worldview

© CA 2019

N. Nader-Rezvani, *An Executive's Guide to Software Quality in an Agile Organization*,
https://doi.org/10.1007/978-1-4842-3751-9_2

Your Dictionary[2]:

- *The overall perspective from which one sees and interprets the world*
- *A collection of beliefs about life and the universe held by an individual or a group*
- *One's personal view of the world and how one interprets it*
- *The totality of one's beliefs about reality*
- *A general philosophy or view of life*

She then continued with the key question of:

What are the elements of worldview?

She had us lay out one hand, palm facing up. Starting with the thumb, we imagined labeling each finger as an element of WV, five in all (i.e., judgment, opinions, biases, beliefs, and values). An easy way to remember this is to call it the JOBB-V. See Figure 2-1. The key idea here is that, just like we have our unique fingerprints, we all have these five elements that make up our own unique WV. Our experiences coupled with the past and present conditions of our life have created this lens.

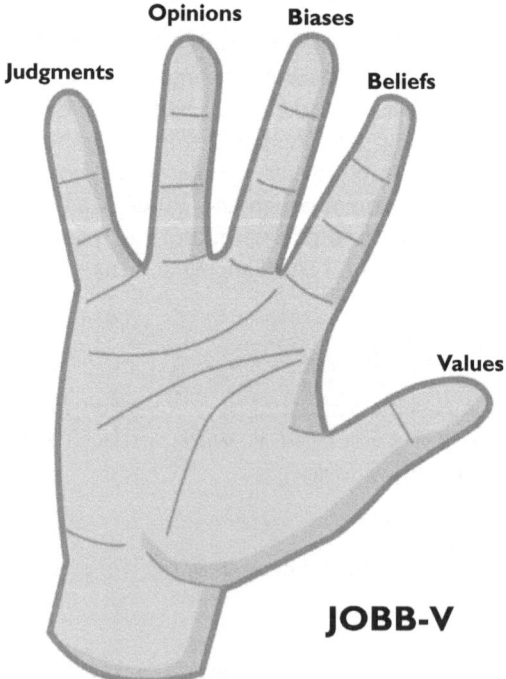

Figure 2-1. Five Elements of Worldview[3]

---

[2]http://www.yourdictionary.com/worldview
[3]Hand graphic by Freepik.com

The next step was to take our hand and lay it palm down on the table. This symbolized that our "JOBB-V" could no longer be seen and taught us that our WV is internal to us. It cannot be seen unless we choose to expose it. We do this through our behaviors and actions.

She used a number of examples to drive home the idea that we all perceive the world differently.

The example she used was a picture of a woman lying down on a bed, face framed with black-rimmed glasses and long blonde hair. Her facial expression was animated. A scrunched-up nose and furrowed brow dominated her features as she stared at the pages of the half-read book in her hand.

What was the story in this picture? Or, more appropriately, what did we each tell ourselves? What story did we make up? As we looked at the picture, and before another word was said, it was evident that our minds were already working overtime as to our assumptions about this person, whom we had never met.

My colleague who was facilitating the WV conversation made a simple yet informative declaration about the woman in the picture. She said, "The summer months are her least favorite time of the year."

With that, the 50 people in the room, including myself, were asked to describe what we perceived from the picture. With only an image and a fact, we quickly formulated our own JOBB-V about this person. Fifty individuals bringing to bear 50 WVs. Everyone came up with a set of judgments, formulated opinions, and in response used their bias and beliefs to guess the person's values and behaviors.

It was eye-opening to learn that the main reason that the woman in the picture disliked the months of summer was that she was an athlete. She was both an Ironman and a serial marathon runner and did not like to train when it was hot and humid. The participants of the workshop had come up with some hypotheses that were quite interesting:

- Perhaps she was lazy and didn't want to leave her house and enjoy long summer days.

- She is not into outdoor physical activities.

- She obviously likes to read books alone and seems antisocial!

- Her face looks pretty red, so she must have a certain illness that prevents her from going outside in the sun.

All of that from looking at just one picture!

As a result of going through that exercise and then discussing the relevance of the concept to teams and organizations undergoing a transformational effort, we came up with the following major takeaways to consider in our journeys:

- **Be self-aware.** Understand and acknowledge that we each carry our own WV that influences how we think, make decisions, and show up in any given situation. We make judgments and form opinions, biases, and beliefs based on our own value system.

- **Know your starting point.** In any transformation, it is critical to know where you are starting from. Where you perceive you are and where you actually are may be different. That also goes for the people and environment around you. Getting calibrated against the big picture will help you make proper priority choices along the way despite roadblocks and challenges.

- **Understand key drivers.** Identify actions that will propel your initiative forward, prioritize which will have the biggest impact, and commit to getting them done.

- **Understand blockers.** As human beings, we have a tendency to focus on things that can't be done or that hold us back. Sometimes, focusing too much on the negatives will overwhelm the team to the point that progress gets impacted or comes to a halt.

- **Measure Success.** Know when it is working and when it is not. Identify smart indicators that keep you focused and ensure you are on the right path.

With respect to engaging with customers, it is important for us to acknowledge that they too will have a worldview. Stepping into that lens creates both awareness and empathy. It helps create more objectivity in areas such as value, challenges, impact, and outcomes from the customers' viewpoint. Pushing our lens beyond our own view is a critical element to success.

Quality Integral Map (QIM)

After covering worldview in the workshop, we moved on to the concept of the Integral Map. WV is a key element in the Integral Theory Model created by Ken Wilber.[4] The Integral Map displays the fusion of key dimensions to how we think and perceive people and the world around us.

---

[4]See https://integrallife.com/four-quadrants/ for the four-quadrant map that is a component of Wilber's Integral Model and see Figure 2-2 for our Integral map.

We learned that the Integral Theory Map helps you see yourself and the world you live in using a holistic or integrated approach. It could certainly be complex and complicated, but it can help you navigate and make better decisions. Being able to create a map to cover all dimensions will give you insight into the various challenges and interdependencies you will encounter along the route of your journey.

Looking for goodness and adding to perspectives are elements that are considered here as well. Remembering that people generally have good intent and don't purposely do things that impact processes and other human beings in a negative way is important. The world needs to be integrated, and our ability to see beyond our differences will allow us to look at challenging issues in a different way so as to resolve them more holistically.

We then started to focus on typical quality-related issues and perceptions from the customers' point of view and began to create a quality map to assess the situation. We referred to it as a Quality Integral Map to focus on the following:

- Worldviews of all individuals involved

- Collective worldviews of all functions involved

- Reflection of individual worldviews and how they are perceived externally

- Conditions and environments that influence the situation

The following example was shared to help us understand the concept better.

Situation:

- An executive leader was very much frustrated with the way issues were getting escalated by a strategic customer.

- The relationship with that customer was getting to be more challenging. They were escalating every issue regardless of its priority.

- The business impact of potentially losing that customer was becoming a major concern for the company as a whole.

Desired State:

- Reduce frustration for both the vendor and customer

- Prevent the customer from moving away and delight them

- Apply the learning to other accounts if applicable

The executive leader started to apply the Worldview and Integral Map concept and worked with his team to:

- Identify all individuals involved that contributed to the situation at hand (including himself) and understand how they saw the problem from their own individual lens

- Identify all collective functions (i.e., Development, Product Management, Sales) involved and their collective worldviews

- Focus on how the situation was being perceived external to the company

- Identify what unique environment and conditions were contributing to the situation and what could be done about them

They continued to zoom in on the details in each of these categories:

- Discussed how all the individuals involved (i.e., the executive himself, developer, support engineer, account manager, customer) possibly contributed to the problem at hand. For example, was it possible that the individuals involved did not take the time to truly understand the issues reported by the customer and perhaps caused collateral damage when providing a new fix? Were best software practices followed (i.e., unit test, end-to-end testing, etc.)? Was the executive himself looking at issues brought up by that customer as isolated incidences and assumed they would get worked on as per proper priority?

- What functions contributed to the collective worldviews (i.e., support team, leadership team, customer account teams, etc.) and how may they have possibly downplayed the issues reported by the customer? Were those functions all feeding off of each other and was the culture changing to where they collectively were not as responsive when issues from that particular customer would show up in their queue? What could a collective approach from all functions be to help the situation?

- What perception was being viewed externally? What was the evidence that created such perceptions?

- Dug deep into the collective set of tickets filed by the customer as well as the responses from his engineering and support engineers back to the customer

- Were the escalations all pointing to a unique root cause or were new fixes being delivered that caused regression?

- Was there proper understanding of the customer's unique use cases?

- Did the documentation reflect the latest changes in the product?

- Paid special attention to what drove the condition and how proper measures could be put in place to avoid future frustrations. How had the circumstances left an impression with the customer and created a perception that quality was not a priority and an integral part of the business for his company?

That thought process helped to open up opportunities for him to work with his team to change their approach in dealing with challenges not only internally or with that one customer, but for their business as a whole.

We then focused on coming up with our own version of the Quality Integral Map for a situation where feedback from customers on product quality was not that great. They were reporting defects that should have been caught internally. As a result, they were not happy with their vendor.

The visual Quality Integral Map that we came up with looked like Figure 2-2.

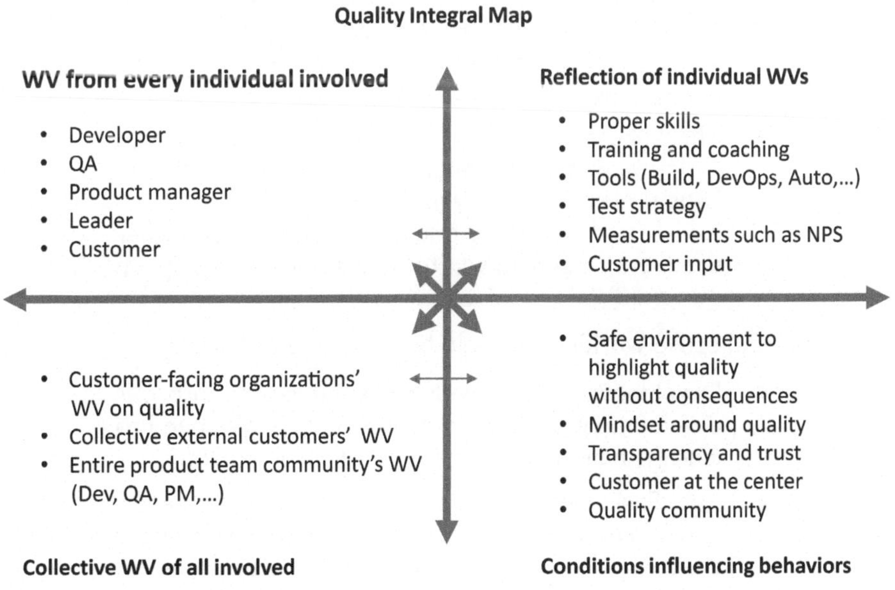

Quality Integral Map

WV from every individual involved

- Developer
- QA
- Product manager
- Leader
- Customer

Reflection of individual WVs

- Proper skills
- Training and coaching
- Tools (Build, DevOps, Auto,...)
- Test strategy
- Measurements such as NPS
- Customer input

- Customer-facing organizations' WV on quality
- Collective external customers' WV
- Entire product team community's WV (Dev, QA, PM,...)

- Safe environment to highlight quality without consequences
- Mindset around quality
- Transparency and trust
- Customer at the center
- Quality community

Collective WV of all involved

Conditions influencing behaviors

Figure 2-2. Quality Integral Map

- Individuals involved in such escalations and their respective worldviews were:

  - Developer – "Unit tests are critical in driving higher code quality. It is important to include writing unit tests in my plan and work estimate."

  - QA Engineer – "Test strategy discussions with the architects, customer-facing organizations, and scrum teams will help me as the Quality Engineer to focus on the highest-priority test scenarios that are most relevant to customers. I will set up time to do so."

  - Engineering leader – "NPS data shows product quality as an area that customers would like to see us improve on. It is important for me to work with the team to create a quality-improvement roadmap to execute against."

  - Support Engineer – "I would like to partner with development to provide feedback and learn about new releases before they go General Availability (GA)."

  - Product Manager – "It is important for me to allow a certain allocation percentage in each release on technical debt improvement and have the team manage their time accordingly."

  - The unhappy customer – "It is key to our success to know that our vendor is focused on quality and issue prevention. Knowing that the product has been fully tested before it reaches us allows for higher productivity and lower total cost of ownership on our end."

- Collective worldviews could be described as follows:

  - Developers – "QA needs to be integrated into our development process to build in quality. We need to engage them from early stages of development."

  - QA Engineers – "It is critical for us to better understand customer use cases and discuss existing challenges with code quality so we can focus on finding issues earlier in the development cycle."

  - Product Management – "We need to follow a consistent model of attending to quality-improvement initiatives by allocating capacity for teams to focus."

- Customers – "We can work collaboratively with the vendor to provide unique use cases that create issues with new releases for us and engage in early validation programs to provide feedback on incremental work."

- Evidence of how the situation was being viewed externally and what could be done to influence the situation in a positive way:

  - Product quality accounts for a high percentage of NPS low scores.

  - Increasing focus on documentation will allow customers to find solutions to low-priority items instead of calling Support for every little issue.

  - Engaging customers in early validation programs will allow for faster feedback and value delivery.

  - Understanding product usage and reviewing customer hot spots should be integrated in the process when test strategy is discussed by the entire team.

- Identified environments and conditions that could have contributed to the situation:

  - Environment needs to be conducive to allowing leadership to have the right mindset and appetite toward quality improvement (I.e., proper reward system is in place, proper organizational structure,…).

  - Ensure there is clarity and agreement among the business leaders (PM) and engineering on technical debt priorities.

  - Think "customer first" in every step of development.

  - Work with the leadership team to ensure there is a culture of transparency and accountability. Creating a safe environment where everyone can speak up without fearing negative consequences is critical.

As you can see, there is a strong interdependency among the four quadrants. The main point here is to consider key elements so as to gain insight into where you are, develop a map to follow, and get to your desired state. All quadrants are interconnected and will help you ask additional questions to get a clear vision of what path to use to get to your defined goal.

Building awareness regarding WV and Quality Integral Map will help with keeping the following important steps in mind, which can lead you through your transformation journey:

- Fully understand and assess where you are today and consider the impact of all internal and external forces in the Quality Integral Map; don't guess!

- Define what success looks like by utilizing available data.

- Be aware of blockers, but focus on enablers.

- Pick the top few quality-impacting factors.

- Prioritize based on the desired outcome.

- Create a plan and get buy-in.

- Establish a transformation team.

- Execute as best as possible.

- Measure and adapt.

- Add new priorities as you gain maturity, and rinse and repeat.

We all have used these thought processes in solving problems. This approach provides a framework to address the issue in a more comprehensive way. Following a Quality Integral Map as a framework will help you identify a path to continue the business and deliver releases while at the same time attending to highlighted challenges that have been ignored in your organization (i.e., Agile adoption, attending to quality technical debt, putting customers at the center, and focusing on holistic quality, to mention a few!).

It is important to acknowledge that we all have a natural disposition to work in one particular quadrant. Perhaps in the quality-related world, we would focus more on evidence that you can see downstream as a result of low quality. With the Quality Integral Map, we need to make sure we consider both internal and external elements in all four quadrants before passing judgment. This model will allow you to validate any hypothesis that you may have created based on the situation at hand. It will help guide you to make wiser decisions.

Having awareness about our worldview, being able to create an Integral Quality Map to gain insight regarding the current state, and prioritizing the actions needed to get to the set vision despite obstacles in the way will be an effective path to success.

Self-Reflection Questions

- Can you relate your worldview to a particular situation you have been in where you perhaps used your personal opinion, biases, or beliefs to pass judgment without having the full context?

- What is the significance of considering internal and external elements when resolving issues?

- Why is it important to know where you are and where you are trying to get to when solving challenging issues?

- Can you relate to the Quality Integral Map discussion in this chapter?

- Can you consider the following situation and describe your thought process to address the situation?

Consider the following situation:

- You have a distributed team.

- The culture of heroism is very much noticed throughout the organization.

- Knowledge sharing and collaboration is not encouraged.

- Meetings are taken over by the people in one geographical location and everyone talks over each other.

Can you use the concept of Quality Integral Map to look at the issue from all angles to identify the best path to this desired state?

- Team members respect each other and collaborate to solve problems together.

- Teams work on preventing issues and do not come to save the day as a hero and get recognized.

- They feel free to express feelings and ideas.

Hint: First, identify all involved individuals and their WV. Then, identify collective internal views, continue with how individual WVs are perceived, and discuss the role of environment and conditions that may possibly need to change.

Perception of Quality

Holistic Quality Is What Matters

Built-in quality is expected and is listed as a table stake in Agile, yet many organizations don't have a solid quality platform or a roadmap for continuously improving on what is so relevant to customers and their success. When I asked various leaders in an organization what quality meant to them, they immediately responded with "Quality is all about defects." I had one executive who offered to stop releasing on all product lines and assign every member of the team to close defects that had been comfortably resting in the product backlogs for many years! The executive was basically saying that teams can only work on features or quality initiatives at any given time, not both. While I was happy that the executive at least was thinking about one aspect of quality, I had to explain why this was not a sustainable model.

Such bug squashes may work temporarily to help resolve issues and reduce anxiety among a few frustrated customers; however, over time the defect backlog will get built back up again—unless the culture and mindset around quality changes within the organization. Also, delivering new features and solutions to stay competitive is expected by customers. Focusing on long bug-squash cycles without innovating new and relevant value to customers could negatively impact a market that expects innovation from their strategic vendors/partners. These types of mutually exclusive approaches toward new functionality and quality are harmful and unwarranted.

© CA 2019
N. Nader-Rezvani, *An Executive's Guide to Software Quality in an Agile Organization*,
https://doi.org/10.1007/978-1-4842-3751-9_3

I like to emphasize how having customers find defects not only lowers their perception of quality, but also costs tens and maybe even hundreds of times more than finding the issues internally and earlier in the lifecycle. Customers are not shy about providing feedback and are pretty blunt about their perception of the product and the company if you just take the time to ask and become an empathetic listener.

One customer provided feedback that our company was very reactive. She said that they didn't normally have any challenges with respect to the responsiveness of our support team when they reported an issue. What they didn't appreciate about our company was the fact that they never got a satisfactory answer when they asked why such issues were not prevented internally to start with. It wasn't clear to her whether proper preventive measures were put in place to avoid similar instances in the future. As a result, they were not convinced that quality was a priority for our company. This really hurt!

Another perception of quality became clear when I spoke with a customer who was furious with the fact that they had called the support organization for a critical issue impacting their production. After being passed around on the call and talking to various junior-level support engineers, she was asked to hold on for a more senior engineer on the team to return from lunch and help with the issue! The senior engineer arrived and resolved the issue in a short amount of time, and she was thankful for that. However, she was still questioning the quality of the service that she received and pointed out that dealing with incompetent and less-skilled people on the phone had cost her company hours of downtime. She went on to point out that they believed our company did not invest in the internal team to ensure proper debugging tools were available. Her company also felt that an insufficient level of training was provided to the employees. That was the main reason why she had given us a low mark on the NPS product quality question.

An important aspect of quality is attending to data privacy and security. News about security breaches has gotten even more attention since the start of the digital transformation and the increased use of mobile devices for many critical online applications (i.e., banking, health-related data handling, etc.). The mindset that software gets inspected at the end of the development cycle should change. Companies have started to realize the importance of integrating security into their development and operations processes and pay more attention to ways that they can weave regular code scanning into the software development process. Data shows that integrating regular scans and identifying and addressing vulnerabilities as they surface, along with fixing other functional defects, could actually allow for establishing a regular release cadence.

In the old software development world, security-code scanning was done later in the development cycle. As a result, the discovery of critical security vulnerabilities late in the development cycle would create a lot of anxiety among the product team members and the business leaders. Release deadlines often put pressure on the product teams to move forward with the planned GA date even while vulnerabilities in the software were not fully addressed. In today's digital world, such compromises are not acceptable by our customers. Putting customers at risk by shipping products with known vulnerabilities is certainly viewed as poor quality by them.

One other customer highlighted that our sales team was the most engaged team they had experienced, until the deal was closed and they were made the proud owner of the purchased solution. But after installing the software and running into issues that needed support, or later on when challenged with upgrading to the latest version, or when making specific enhancement requests, their support tickets were not getting much traction. They initially went back to the extremely engaged sales team that they had dealt with originally, but were told to go through the normal support channels as they were not responsible after the initial sale!

A customer who had participated in a beta program, spending many hours evaluating a new version of the software and providing valuable feedback, was upset about the vendor's response. He was told that while his input was valuable, due to time constraints, the team could not include changes in the current scheduled release. Even for future releases, he was told that his feedback would get prioritized against other planned fixes and enhancements and would be processed accordingly. He was not happy that he had taken lots of time to provide detailed feedback and was basically told thanks but no thanks! That was poor quality, in his mind!

We had frustrated customers as a result of our adoption of Agile. They were told that Agile was being adopted internally and that Agile calls for a lean system. As part of implementing Agile, teams reduced the extent of their documentation. As a result, the release notes and known-issues list did not reflect all the details that users needed to be able to maneuver through and debug the issue. Customers were forced to call support, create a ticket, and wait a long time for a response.

Raw responses from surveys that were sent to customers provided invaluable insight into how customers view quality as a whole. The responses clearly reflected that customers make key long-term business investment decisions based on their perception of quality. It is important to highlight that keeping loyal customers and helping them stay current is just as important as (or even more important than) attracting new customers. Building in quality will allow for "trapped customers" to become "loyal customers".

Customer acquisition versus retention is not a new concept. Studies show that the cost of acquiring a new customer is anywhere from four to five times higher that of retaining an existing customer. Yet, many companies focus a big portion of their efforts on acquiring new customers. Internalizing this concept was a wakeup call in one of the companies that I was at.

The concept of having loyal customers rather than trapped customers is very relevant to the lifecycle management discussion. As part of the consulting work that I did for a Fortune 500 company, we started to focus on a SWOT (Strengths, Weaknesses, Opportunities, Threats) analysis to create a starting point for our effort. In one of the early meetings, the business leader for the organization included "having many customers trapped with our solutions" under the Strength quadrant! I thought he was trying to include some humor for the meeting. I laughed when he read that bullet, but no one else was smiling!

I immediately realized that they were confusing customer loyalty with customers' being trapped with their solutions. Having their solutions be heavily integrated in their customers' infrastructure gave them a level of comfort; customers would put up with all of their shortcomings (i.e., product quality) because it would be difficult to rip out their solution and go with another vendor! Fast forward to a couple of years after that discussion, when the vendor lost one of their strategic customers. This customer had given the vendor many warnings and requested (at times begged) for better quality around upgrades, but were ignored. While switching vendors was very painful and costly for the customer, they had finally reached their tolerance threshold and were done accepting the shortcomings of the original vendor.

Who Contributes to the Product Quality?

As we saw in earlier examples,

- quality is not limited to test-case execution or defect tracking;

- the total customer experience (TCE) is what is perceived as total quality; and

- everyone in the organization contributes to the overall quality perceived by customers.

Figure 3-1 shows major functions that exist in most product development teams. They all play a role in ensuring customers' perception of quality is high.

Figure 3-1. Functions that contribute to quality

The main message here is that building a quality product can be a daunting task when only a few people in the organization are expected to be responsible for it. It is very important that everybody in the organization is kept informed and shares the same understanding of the quality improvement plan. That will ensure every action of theirs, from the conception of idea to product delivery, to customer deployment, to sales and support, is aligned toward meeting the quality objectives of the organization. Open communication, common information, and a sense of shared accountability are key to building an organization with a built-in quality culture. Quality and Continuous Process Improvement (CPI) must be engraved in the DNA of the organization as a whole!

To align company's culture with their strategic quality objectives, leadership team in one organization selected their top quality-impacting categories and set reasonable milestones along the way to achieving the specific goals highlighted in each category (see Figure 3-2). This took a lot of coordination, education, learning, and unlearning by cross-functional teams. Striking a balance to keep the focus on major quality-impacting categories while ensuring innovation by releasing new features was difficult. But once the mindset was changed around quality and new technical debt was not being introduced, it actually helped the organization achieve their goals.

Key Initiatives to Support Quality Objectives

Focus on enhancing internal software development best practices to increase quality of solutions for our customers and address their pain points with higher velocity

CATEGORY	Highest Priority Initiatives & Rationale/Desired Outcomes

Reduce TCO	▪ <u>Partner with customer-facing organizations to prioritize customer pain points:</u>
	   ▪ Develop plans to address:
	      ▪ Installability -- Ensure new installs will uninstall successfully followed by re-install
	      ▪ Integrability -- Create an environment to validate integration of multiple products
	      ▪ Upgradability -- Establish a process to do internal successful automated upgrades
	      ▪ Securability -- Integrate Securability tools into our development processes
	      ▪ Review early warnings and hot spots regularly and continuously improve

VOTC	▪ <u>Incorporate voice of the customers in product development processes</u>
	   ▪ Active participation from internal and external customers at the end of sprints
	   ▪ Exploratory validation by all internal customers after exiting each sprint
	   ▪ Dev/Buddy program where customers meet with product teams to provide feedback

Address Tech Debt	▪ <u>Invest in Automation</u> ▪ Assess test coverage and automate the highest ROI impacting ones first to deliver fixes to customers faster and increase new release and CR cadence ▪ <u>Architecture simplification (i.e., invest in Restful APIs, code cleanup, and modularization/modernization)</u> ▪ <u>Focus on certifications and out of date third-party software</u>

Figure 3-2. Example of key initiatives to support product quality

The leadership team then started to go deeper into each of the areas by asking a few important questions in order to figure out the next immediate steps:

- What is our target condition?

- What is our actual condition now?

- What obstacles are there that prevent us from getting to our target condition? Which one can be addressed first?

- What should be our next logical step?

- What is the best way to measure our success along the way?

After several discussions at the leadership level where they considered the responses from the cross-functional organizations to the preceding questions, they identified their next immediate steps:

1. Form a team to focus on assessing:

   - Total cost of ownership (TCO) / Net Promoter Score (NPS) high-priority impacting factors (i.e., deployment, upgradability, integration, number of hot fixes per customer)

- Test coverage for effectiveness and automatability
- Code coverage and continuous integration of code for higher quality
  - Automation percentage increase in most-popular functionalities
  - Monitored leading and lagging indicators to measure success
- Percentage of successful deployments/upgrades/integration issues (often measured by the number of support calls made during such operations)
- Reduction in number of hot fixes per customer per quarter
- Volume drivers trend in known areas
- Factors contributing to high defect density

2. After establishing the team and digging deeper into key issues, they came up with an overall strategy that was presented across the entire organization, and calls for action were made. See Figure 3-3.

Quality Strategic Summary

Vision: Deliver simple solutions to our customers that have been validated internally to solve their problems on time and on quality.

Strategic Objectives		
• Invest in areas that prevent us from delivering releases on regular cadence • Retrain in Agile for all • Prioritize customer pain points and build internal infrastructure to deliver against them in future releases	• Deliver service packs at a regular cadence • Invest in CI/CD • Build integrated environment, utilize customer configuration and data to validate upgrade, installation, deployment	• Expand practices to all other Product Teams • Voice of the customers in every development phase • Focus on SaaS-specific needs • Automate solution validation of customer configurations

Figure 3-3. Example of a Quality Strategic Objective for an organization

Specific Solutions to Overcome Key Quality Challenges

In addition to the areas that have been discussed so far, a few more played significant roles in enhancing quality and addressing customer needs.

Streamlining Platform Support Matrix (PSM)

One major area that seemed to be a common challenge faced by various teams was the large platform support matrix (PSM). Over the years, no attempt was made to deprecate older platforms, operating systems, browser versions, and databases. As a result, customers expected new releases to be backward compatible with many different versions. This was causing quality challenges, as certifying so many different configurations was not scalable.

I did a simple calculation for one product line based on the possible permutation of various OS, browsers, databases, and platforms and came up with 4,000,000 combinations. Yes, that was based on a simple math calculation. I shared that data with our support and sales teams to emphasize that there was no way that the product teams could validate all possible combinations internally. A logical approach was to team up with customer-facing organizations to get better data and come up with a realistic plan to ensure validated combinations reached our customers.

I did some investigation and came up with three distinct areas, as shown in Figure 3-4, from which information needed to be captured to help streamline the PSM matrix:

- Most common and popular configurations used by customers
- Configurations that had generated the most number of support calls
- The industry trend on supporting various combinations and configurations

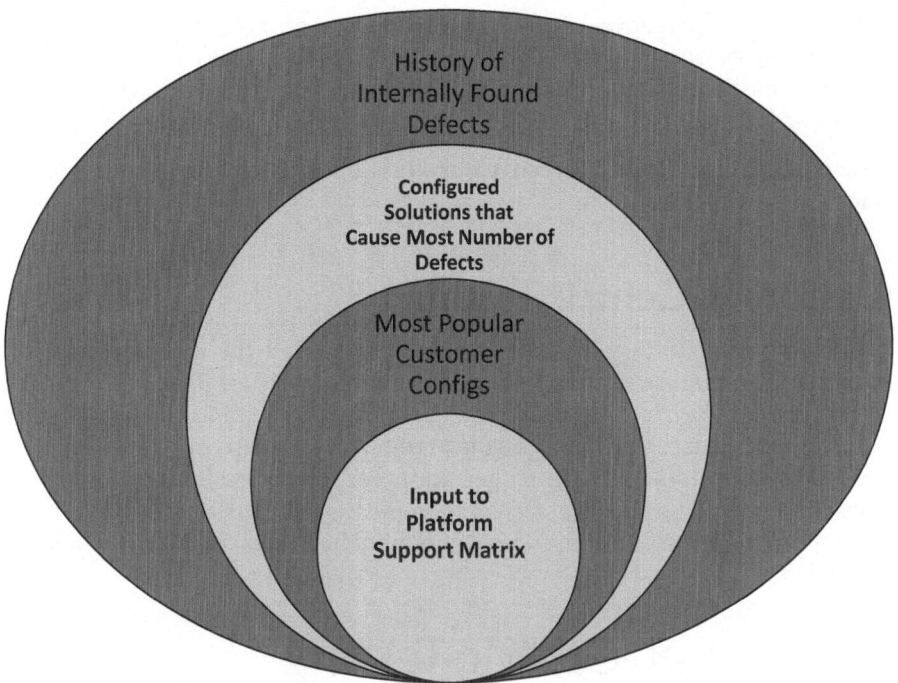

Figure 3-4. Factors that contribute in streamlining platform support matrix

Supported Versus Certified

Putting the focus on streamlining PSM as an important quality-impacting factor, allowed for innovative ideas to bubble up. Analyzing support data, presales' input on the new market trends, and professional services' input on common challenges seen with specific configurations allowed us to define the concept of support versus certified.

We agreed on five critical reference architectures by which to continuously validate new software during the release cycle; we referred to these as "certified" configurations. All others were reviewed from the architectural point of view and were considered as "supported," meaning if customers ran into issues, they could still contact our support organization for help. It also allowed us to perform proper business and cost analysis to decide which key reference architectures to focus on.

Over time, sales and other customer-facing departments would encourage customers to migrate their infrastructure to one of the five reference architectures that were fully certified internally. This was a huge win and a major quality-improvement factor. Also, product management started to allow for the deprecation of platforms that were no longer as popular with the majority of our customers. Such sensitive conversations took place with impacted customers in order to minimize surprises and perceived quality-impacting factors.

This process was later referred to as "Navid's Law of Horrific Reference Stack!"

Customer-Centric Testing

In addition, test strategy was something that needed the organization's full attention. The culture of customer-centric testing (Figure 3-5) and metrics-driven testing (Figure 3-6) did not exist in the organization. The policy of ensuring every customer issue got a full review and a deep root-cause analysis was performed, took a while to get adopted. Great results were achieved once the entire organization started to implement it. Customers were much happier with the releases and loved the fact that their input was making a difference.

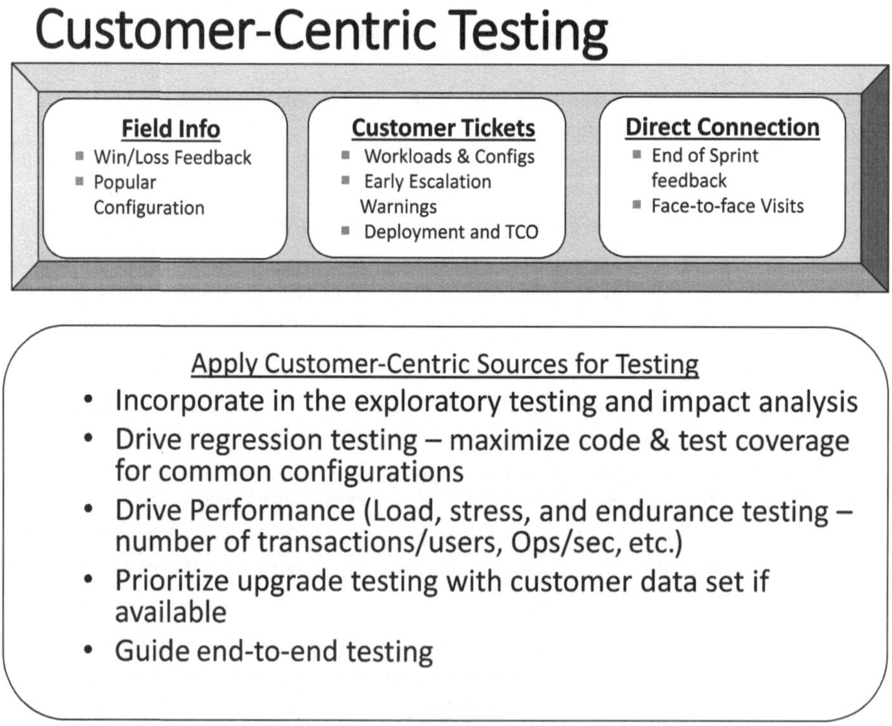

Customer-Centric Testing

Field Info	Customer Tickets	Direct Connection
■ Win/Loss Feedback ■ Popular Configuration	■ Workloads & Configs ■ Early Escalation Warnings ■ Deployment and TCO	■ End of Sprint feedback ■ Face-to-face Visits

Apply Customer-Centric Sources for Testing
- Incorporate in the exploratory testing and impact analysis
- Drive regression testing – maximize code & test coverage for common configurations
- Drive Performance (Load, stress, and endurance testing – number of transactions/users, Ops/sec, etc.)
- Prioritize upgrade testing with customer data set if available
- Guide end-to-end testing

Figure 3-5. Sources for customer-centric testing

Testing Driven by Various Metrics

Code-coverage metrics
Test-execution reports
Defect-tracking data

__Metrics Considered__	__Quality Analysis__
1. Code coverage to resolve test/automation gaps	1. Test coverage analysis as per the test management documented info
2. Code coverage to optimize regression testing	2. Defect trend for code health measurements (incoming vs. fixed)
3. Defect trending and regression analysis to guide testing in Hardening phase	3. Overall performance dashboards

Figure 3-6. Testing driven by measuring key metrics

Root Cause and Corrective Action (RCCA) of Customer Issues

Another major improvement in addressing customer issues and avoiding building additional technical debt was to revisit our support cases and the ones that required L2 support. By performing the steps shown below, we were able to significantly improve our quality.

- Carefully perform RCCA (Root Cause and Corrective Action) by analyzing each issue, understanding the impact and root cause, and coming up with the corrective action.

- Reproduce the issue and identify the required fix.

- Update test cases and automation of test suites.

- Validate changes in the main branch before backporting it into the reported maintenance branch.

- Document details and respond back to the customer.

Self-Reflection Questions

1. Why is the perception of quality important?

2. Who is responsible for quality in an organization?

3. Can you describe the difference between accountability and responsibility?

4. Why does streamlining the product support matrix improve quality?

5. How do you define customer-centric and metric-driven testing?

6. What is the role of RCCA in elevating quality?

7. Can you describe trapped versus loyal customers?

8. Why is it important to focus on retaining customers?

Quality Challenges in an Agile Team

Real-World Examples

This chapter will include examples of teams that have embarked on quality journeys so as to address various challenges, change their culture, and deliver solutions to customers in a predictable manner. As I mentioned before, Agile processes assume that certain quality disciplines are integrated in the culture of an organization. For example, having a continuous regression automated test suite and an effective build process is assumed. In many organizations, I have witnessed teams struggle with basic value delivery due to lack of quality disciplines.

Examples in this chapter come from real product teams and organizations that got trained and believed themselves to be Agile, yet saw their product quality continue to suffer. Reflecting on the Quality Integral Map and performing a value-stream analysis provided visibility into where the challenges were and helped those teams look at all angles to find the best approach to resolving the

© CA 2019
N. Nader-Rezvani, *An Executive's Guide to Software Quality in an Agile Organization*,
https://doi.org/10.1007/978-1-4842-3751-9_4

issues at hand. Only then were specific objectives achieved. Most step-by-step processes that were followed by the teams can be used by any organization in any type of industry to continuously improve quality, elevate customer satisfaction, and eventually increase revenue.

Product Team Example 1

Key focus areas:

- Reduce long tail (hardening phase) and gain predictable release cycle:
  - Build proper automation framework
  - Develop a solid performance-testing strategy
  - Streamline platform support matrix (PSM)
- Invest in people and promote good software-development practices.
- Reduce escalations and escaped defects.
- Improve customer satisfaction.

I was once hired into a fairly large organization as the head of the Quality Engineering (QE) team. My interview with the chief architect for the product team was an interesting one. He told me that he wasn't convinced they needed a head of Quality Engineering and asked me to explain to him the reason why a head of QE role was even needed. I obviously was a bit surprised by that question. But, I managed to get myself together quickly and responded: "If you and the development team have a quality mindset, stop putting the defects in, and start thinking like customers, you wouldn't need me or any of the QE members to act as customer advocates." There was a long and awkward silence in the room!

In talking to the rest of the leadership team during my interview at that company, I was reminded repeatedly about the number of hours every team had spent in training classes with external vendors to learn Agile. In fact, I was told that they considered themselves a mature team in the world of Agile, but were puzzled as to why they were still getting low quality marks on their customer survey!

I ended the interview and came home to share with my family that all my interviews went well, but that I didn't score well with the chief architect, who was one of the key decision makers in the business unit. To my surprise, I was offered the position! Later on, I was told by the chief architect that the answer I'd given really struck a chord with him. Changing the culture and thinking of

QE as a partner and not a separate function responsible for identifying flaws in a faulty code was the correct mindset to establish in the organization. He later became my biggest ally when I needed to implement new quality-enhancing processes.

Once I came on board and started to talk to the rest of the team members, I got different views that didn't quite match what I had heard during my interview. For example, I heard that the team hadn't released a major release of software for over three years. They also shared how a release that the entire organization had worked hard on was stopped during the last stages of the release, very close to their GA date. No one could articulate the reason other than the fact that features were not valuable to customers. That realization was shared with the team right as they were starting the final stages of their hardening cycle! You can imagine the negative impact canceling that release had on the team's morale.

I also sensed a bit of a tension between development and the QE organization, where with every customer escalation, QE was being put under the microscope as to why they had missed finding that issue internally. Learning more about the team's dynamics provided more insight into why the chief architect had reservations about my role and asked me the question regarding the need for the QE leader!

When I joined the team, they were focusing on the last stages of development of features committed for a new release. Excited about finally joining a team that at least knew the ABCs of Agile, I showed up to work and attended the very first global product team meeting, which consisted of all the scrum masters (14 of them), head of engineering, head of product management, program manager, product owners, and architects.

Observing the Team Dynamics

The first thing I noticed was that the majority of the discussion, questions, and suggestions were coming from the US-based teams and very little was said over the phone from teams in other global locations. The meeting was conducted in the morning US time. Perhaps either it was too late in the evening in the other locations and people were left with little energy to speak or the culture was such that their viewpoints were not considered and so they didn't bother speaking. I didn't know which one was true at the time.

I had attended the meeting just to observe and learn. A few important dates and milestones were shared that I took note of. Mind you, I was still very unfamiliar with the people, culture, language, tools, and processes used in the organization. The key takeaway from that meeting was that all discussions were referencing a date that was eight weeks away to go GA and wrap up all the details that were needed to do so.

Listening a bit more, I also learned from references to running performance tests and upgrading from the prior versions that these were areas that were yet to be worked on. I started to get a bit uneasy, but perhaps I didn't know all the details. Then, I learned about the significant number of open defects, details that needed to be worked out for the beta program, and a few other details that got me really concerned.

After the meeting, I asked one of the engineers on my team to show me the tool(s) they were using to track their release and specific sprints to get a better understanding of what was done and what was remaining. I watched him log into various tools and struggle with explaining the current status as updates were not clearly reflected in any of the tools. Burn up/down charts, status of defects, link to the performance plan, feature details, and other relevant information were not easily consumable.

At that point, I was panicking!

A logical thing for me to do was to connect with my manager to better understand his vision and objectives. After all, he clearly knew that the team had been struggling to release software for a couple of years, and as far as I could tell from attending that meeting, they were still struggling with the current version of the release.

The next day, I got invited to the Release Leadership Team meeting, where the decision makers were all getting together to discuss the latest release status. The program manager started the meeting by reminding everyone of the GA date that was set for eight weeks from then. She also introduced me again and reminded everyone of my role as the quality leader.

She then walked everyone through the standard status update that went something like this:

- One round of regression tests is 70 percent complete.
- 250 must-fix defects are open and the team is doing a great job addressing them.
- Many hours are spent in debugging intermittent automation failures, but team is making some progress.
- Performance testing setup is near completion to begin testing.
- Beta-testing announcement is being worked on. The start date was proposed to be set for two weeks from then (six weeks from GA!)

A few other updates were made, but I wasn't listening anymore, as I was trying to digest how, with such a release update, anyone could feel comfortable releasing in eight weeks. I thought for sure everyone would start objecting to the dates considering the updates. I waited a bit, but to my surprise everyone seemed comfortable with the milestones and were ready to wrap up the meeting.

At that point, I had to break my silence and started off by introducing myself again and my role and reminded everyone that the quality of the release was my main concern, as I was sure it was for everyone else on the release team. I had a lot of questions about the status that was just shared. I asked if I could sit down with someone to go over those questions or if it was ok to bring them up in that forum. Everyone wanted to hear them. So, I started with some simple questions as follows:

- **What percentage of the regression test is manual?**

  Answer: Because we have had many issues with our UI-based automation, we have been relying mostly on the manual testing, so close to 100 percent.

- **Asked about the incoming and fix rates of issues as a result of the completed regression test**

  Answer: Incoming rate has far exceeded the fix rate in the last few iterations, but it is expected since regression testing is in progress.

  The defect chart showed with that rate, it would take six more months to get to zero defects, assuming no new issues bubbled up!

- **How much effort has been put into fixing the automation failures, and do you see any value in debugging further?**

  Answer: Many hours with inconclusive results. Team had been struggling to see the value of thousands of tests that were automated. Since that release had a huge focus on redoing the UI, the existing UI-based automation framework had been badly broken.

- **Was there any prior performance testing done at the server side to be used as a reference?**

  Answer: Some available results are inconsistent. The team is now setting up an isolated environment since the results we had before were from a shared environment, where functional testing and performance use cases were being run on the same machine and at the same time.

- **Has there been any specific customer scenario testing to validate new features against?**

  Answer: None that PM has provided

- At that point, I just asked a simple question of: **Does anyone else feel as uncomfortable as I feel or are there other points that I am missing? The eight weeks to GA and two weeks to beta both seem risky to me.**

  Answer: If you think about it that way, we can see why it seems scary for someone new to the organization, but our team is very strong and they will/have been putting a lot of long hours. They don't want to have another unsuccessful release either, and we are confident that they will pull through.

I came out of that meeting feeling not so well. I felt like calling it a day and going home early and was thinking to myself: "What have I gotten myself into?" I needed a lot more info, and it was hard to decide where to start with so many unanswered questions. I needed to become the program manager's new best friend to learn more details!

I also scheduled many sessions with key engineers, product owners, scrum masters, and support engineers. Those sessions were extremely valuable. It was then that things started to make sense and fall in place for me. Everyone that I spoke with had their reservations and was skeptical on the set GA date. They were working off of daily tasks and were ignoring the longer milestones because they knew they couldn't work more hours in a day or sacrifice any more family time than they already had. None of the basic Agile principles were being followed. In fact, even daily standups were not being held for some teams because they were "too busy" to break for them!

Other important areas that I captured information on were:

- Automation framework
- Regression-testing strategy
- Build process
- Branching strategy
- Performance-testing approach
- Design implementation as per available requirements
- Competing priorities among various product owners

I also learned that QE did not have a strong voice. In fact, on certain occasions they were not included in discussions regarding determining the work estimate. That was because every time QE was invited, they would point out additional areas to focus on and reasons why the required effort wouldn't fit in the allocated time. Or, as I had heard it before, "They had a problem for every solution offered!"

It was extremely helpful to sit through various scrum-team discussions, talk to the individuals and first-line managers, and get access to the defect tracking and test case management systems.

I spent the first few days collecting all that data. Time was running out, and I knew I had to compile a list of key points to share with my manager, who seemed not to be aware of all the low-level challenges that team members were faced with. In fact, he was getting ready to engage with beta customer candidates to unveil the big release date. I knew I had to do something, but also knew well that by declaring war with the Release Leadership Team, I wouldn't be successful or gain their support in the long run. I needed a different strategy and lots of luck!

At the end of the first week, there was enough info that I could share with my manager. He was excited to hear what I had observed and what I had to say. I started by complimenting the team and their desire to do the right thing. But I was also curious to know how closely he was watching the release and if he was even aware of certain challenges that weren't necessarily coming up in various forums that he was attending.

When he started to show his excitement about the beta program and how he was getting ready to announce the release availability, I knew my message would be hard for him to digest. He went on by saying how he valued the long hours that the team was putting in to meet the date. It was pretty obvious that he hadn't internalized all the release details and risk signals, or he was a bit out of the loop. In further discussing the release details, it became apparent that while he knew deep inside how quality needed to be paid attention to, it wasn't a priority for him or the sales team that he was engaged with.

I was careful not to crush his view of the release immediately and decided to state some facts and watch his reaction. That would be a good initial indication of what I could expect on my road ahead with that organization. After all, it was important for me to understand if quality was truly on anyone's mind.

High-Level Release Status

So, here is how, at the high level, I summarized my observations after a short time with the team:

- The release team is bullish about the release date and believes in the GA date's being viable despite many open areas that I have learned about.

- Individual team members have a different view, and, despite all the hard work they are putting in, they don't see the light at the end of the tunnel.

- Team members are exhausted and getting frustrated and disappointed, especially after their prior experience with an unsuccessful release. They don't want the same thing to happen again this time around.

- Not everyone on the scrum team is informed of the overall release status, and critical metrics are not obvious to all. As a result, informed decisions are not always being made.

- Teams are working in silos; integration of work is a topic that is being discussed in pockets and not as a whole.

- Defect data doesn't add up, and pure math doesn't justify the current GA release date.

- Basic Agile principles are being violated despite the fact that extensive trainings have been conducted.

- Non-functional testing is yet to begin (i.e., performance, upgradability, accessibility, etc.).

- US teams are more engaged, but dependencies on other geographical locations are not openly discussed and mitigated.

- Manual testing provides a huge risk to the release date given the number of incoming defects, closure rate, and the fact that many of the non-functional testing efforts are yet to begin and will possibly generate more complex defects. Those complex issues could possibly need major fixes that require many cycles of manual regression testing that could take away many cycles/hours from the team.

- Questions about functionality and ambiguity regarding detailed requirements are coming up late in the release cycle and could put at risk the adoption of new features by customers.

- Having the beta date so close to the GA will run the risk of customers spending valuable time reporting issues and us not being able to fix them in time because we are too close to wrapping up the release and don't have enough time to fix them

Before I could get to my complete list, his excitement and happy face were fading away. He said while he had seen bits and pieces of such info, he had not seen a compiled list of issues the way it was being presented to him to make a full assessment and decide accordingly with the rest of his staff.

That was an important viewpoint from someone who had just joined the organization, he added. Everyone was so consumed with the release activities and daily tasks that they didn't have the time to stop and look at collective list of dependencies, challenges, and obstacles for the entire release and not individual teams. He was appreciative of the unfiltered viewpoint that I had shared with him. However, he was not too excited to hear that based on what I had observed, the team needed at least a few more months to get to GA; that is, if everything aligned well and no new surprises showed up!

Product Team Leader's Action

He decided to call a meeting with the Release Team members to go over the status and challenges and ask the team to put a more realistic plan in place. He could then communicate a new date with Sales and other departments that were expecting a quality release in less than eight weeks.

During the next Release Team meeting, we asked all members to bring visibility to the challenges that they each knew about. The objective was to get the team to agree on the overall impact of the individual challenges and come to an agreement that the current GA and beta dates were not feasible.

After reviewing the preceding list and additional items that others brought up as potential risks, we collectively acknowledged that with the current state of the release, there was no way we could achieve the set milestones and still deliver a minimum viable product that would excite our customers and leave a good impression with them. We needed short-and long-term plans to address all known quality issues.

Our business-unit leader took the initiative to alert the Sales partners of the recent development and asked the Release Team to come back with a plan and new beta and GA dates.

The mindset of the organization was still set in such a way that QE was to blame for many late findings and not completing the regression cycle fast enough. I knew well that I had a lot of work ahead of me. But first things first!

Short-Term Actions

As a starting point, we needed to come together as a Release Team and collectively put the ship back on track. The program manager and I started to meet a couple of times a day. That allowed us to work on a list of must-have items to put in place as a short-term solution to ensure there was transparency across the product team about the state of the release.

I reviewed the following list of changes that were necessary to provide visibility across the teams. The Release Team was very supportive of what was needed:

- Publishing key release radiators/metrics daily that were relevant to that stage of the release for everyone to get better informed

- Working with teams to ensure basic Agile practices were built back into the daily routines

- Revamping daily standups with key objectives around the three key elements: what was accomplished yesterday, what is being done today, and listing impediments and dependencies

- Recording standup sessions for distributed teams if their meetings were at an inconvenient time for other scrum-team members. Expectations were set to listen to those recordings and send clarifying questions back to the remote team.

- Attendance at daily standups for product owners and tech writers was made mandatory. Every member was encouraged to write a list of questions that involved implementation of a story to leave no ambiguity in the design and update DoD in the story itself.

- End-of-sprint demos were taken more seriously, and teams were asked to assess their own success based on what they completed versus what was planned.

- The decision was made to put the overhead of triaging endless automation framework fix efforts on hold with the promise to come up with a long-term plan.

- Updates to the stories were asked to be done daily so the scrum teams could review before the standups and ask relevant questions.

- Capacity for the team was assessed against the planned/completed work for the prior sprints to ensure visibility and realistic commitment by teams.

- A sprint dashboard was created to provide transparency on the team's success against their planned effort, remaining regression, defect status, blocking issues, and dependencies on other teams.

- The "done" criteria for stories, defects, features, and release were reviewed and republished as a reminder to all. Posters were made and put in visible locations.

- Non-functional challenges were highlighted as risks, and a list of required tiger teams was published to be addressed by the Release Team in the order of priority.

The preceding changes required a realignment for the entire product team. Our product-team leader held a meeting with the entire organization to discuss why it was necessary to take a deeper look at the current state. Accountability and transparency were highlighted as the two key elements that we needed to establish to get to the endgame. Quality was also mentioned as a non-negotiable element, which made me extremely happy!

Initially, I was expecting to not be very popular with the team as a result of highlighting so many challenges and expecting a different level of focus from the teams. But it was refreshing to learn that the majority viewed the reset in the release process as a much-needed step, and the support they provided allowed us to eventually release a product that resonated with customers and generated excitement internally with the team members as well.

A simple set of metrics that were tied to the upcoming milestones in the release were chosen. These short-term metrics allowed us to focus on finishing what was absolutely critical with the right level of urgency to get to the endgame. For example, if the next milestone was to get to the end of the build phase and complete all new features in the release, we used the following simple metrics:

- New and regression-test execution status (pass, fail, remaining)

- Number of must-fix defects (all severities)

- Story points remaining for each team in the specific sprint

Not all the info was readily available, but highlighting them as key metrics allowed for some innovation in automatically capturing most of the required data from various sources. We hired an intern to focus on collecting and publishing such info. That table was created every morning and sent to the entire organization. Every team had visibility into other teams' status, and unknowingly a healthy competition among teams was created, and discussions around the break room started to brew!

In regard to the Agile principles and practices that were needed long term, we all felt that a refresher course was needed. The scrum masters were asked to play a big role there and discuss with their teams how they could best bring some basic principles back. We also elevated the voice of the experienced Agile practitioners in the organization. We were able to borrow some time from a couple of Agile coaches to observe and provide feedback to the teams with minimal disruption and help us create a plan for a longer-term training after the major milestones of the release were accomplished.

There were many other quality elements that we needed to attend to over time. Given our situation with resources and limited budget, we had to prioritize what we needed to go after first. Agile training and practices, automation, and performance seemed the obvious first choices.

Preparing for Long-Term Actions

That feedback was invaluable for when we needed to unlearn certain practices and relearn later. Daily updates to the stories and defect status allowed for a more accurate set of metrics to be published every day. No team wanted to be highlighted in the daily status table as having a red status due to the fact that they were so far off from their planned commitment.

Better Engagement with Global Teams

I took several trips to our other sites. Did I mention that the product had team members in more than 15 locations? Obviously, co-location—highlighted as one of the key disciplines in Agile—was not very well internalized there. We didn't have critical mass in all of those locations, but most of our engineering teams were located in four different geographical time zones. It made it almost impossible to hold an all-team collaboration session without someone being inconvenienced. Meeting with our team members globally and truly understanding their challenges allowed us to make certain changes such as:

- running more effective meetings
- engaging product owners in all scrum team meetings
- holding regular backlog grooming sessions with the entire team including the product owners
- conducting regular inspect and adapt session

For example, instead of holding end-of-sprint demos every two weeks during the early morning hours in the United States and late afternoon in India and very late evening hours in the Far East, we decided to share the pain and rotate the end-of-sprint demo time. Such little changes created a culture that showed we cared about each global team equally. That feeling didn't exist before, and in fact in my discussions with the oversees team members they complained about the inconveniently scheduled EoS demos and how hard it was to manage that for their local team. I refer to addressing this issue as the *Law of Engaging Global Teams*.

Promoting DoD & DoR

It was also interesting that despite having published Definition of Done (DoD) and Definition of Ready (DoR) on the internal wiki, no one reviewed those regularly. In fact, the engineer that I went to couldn't find the link to show it to me. Many stories were written without an acceptance criteria and had a one-line description at best. It was unclear if that story was even ready to be picked up. Yet, teams would start on such stories and often made assumptions when they were faced with functionality questions and didn't have access to the product owner—or details were not even discussed by or known to the product owner either.

Figure 4-1 shows the minimal list of DoD and DoR that I worked with the teams to come up with and ensure there was buy-in to be followed. I printed out the list and had teams post it in their team gathering areas globally. Over time and as teams gained more Agile maturity and quality became a strong part of the culture, we updated the initial list and created a more comprehensive list.

DoR	DoD for Story	DoD for Feature	DoD for Release
Clear objective of the feature/story and business value	Acceptance criteria met, code reviewed	Success criteria met including non-functional tests	All features accepted by PM
Clear acceptance criteria	Tests executed and automated as per plan; no regression	All stories for the feature accepted; no regression	All planned test execution complete with no regression (including E2E)
Customer use case/UX documented	Automated tests run successfully in CI/CD	Feature successfully demoed, integrated, and accepted by PM	Zero new defects and no must-fix defects
Non-functional requirements captured		Feature is documented and reviewed	All non-functional areas covered and issues addressed along with certifications (e.g., VPAT, security scan, localization,etc.)

Figure 4-1. *An Example of DoR and DoD*

Defect Severity and Priority

Another area that had created anxiety and a source of conflict among development and QE was the severity and priority of issues. We decided to go based on the standard severity definitions, but use priority as a more important factor to decide what issues to fix first. The idea was that even if the severity of an issue was low, if in the customers' view it was considered annoying enough to generate a support call, we would mark it with a higher priority to ensure it got resolved. Support became a great partner in this effort to review issues that needed priority clarification from the customers' point of view. Analyzing impact and likelihood of each defect provided an opportunity to prioritize issues with higher confidence.

We also decided that for new features, we would address all known issues, or, if there was a decision against fixing a very low severity/priority issue, the team would collectively discuss and decide against fixing it and close it with the appropriate comments. That would allow teams to really think through the impact and likelihood of the issue, and by resolving it as "will not fix" it wouldn't add to the defect backlog. Basically, we wanted to do no harm and at the minimum didn't want to build any additional technical debt.

Initial Steps for Operationalizing Automation

The automation situation needed a lot more focus. We started to get the senior-and architect-level developers and QE together to discuss the current framework and plan a longer-term solution. I came to learn that after challenges faced with the existing UI-based framework, where over 12,000 test cases were automated, a more solid and headless automation framework infrastructure had already been designed by a couple of engineers, but they did not have time to complete it and operationalize it. That was my opportunity to take what was done, get another review done by the architects, and put plans in place to operationalize it for future releases.

Since the current framework was put on hold due to the level of effort needed to debug test scripts that were failing intermittently, every QE was tasked with manually executing tests. When I asked a few engineers about the process they were following to decide on what tests to run for the newly developed features as well as the regression of existing features, I didn't get the warm and fuzzy feeling that people knew what was needed. There was no common test strategy being followed as far as I could tell.

In fact, I was told many times that in Agile, there is no time to document test cases, and in an iteration, there is not always enough time to ensure there is no regression to existing features. As a result, they were hoping to run through the entire regression suite in their hardening phase. But the required analysis to determine if it was even possible to run through the entire test suite during the hardening phase had not been done. A simple back-of-the-envelope analysis led me to believe that it would take over six months even if every scrum team member was assigned to execute them all!

This was a big concern, as in Agile having an automated regression-test framework is assumed. If you are to develop features with a regular cadence and with a set velocity, it is important to have continuous regression automated test suites running to ensure existing functionalities are not negatively impacted once new features are developed. Customers get really upset when they upgrade to a new version of software and an existing functionality is no longer working properly.

We spent a lot of time thinking about how to fix this issue. This was not something that QE alone could tackle. It required an investment in both tools and people. Given the fact that the team hadn't released software for quite some time, business leaders (PM) were not exactly in the mood to give out additional money to the development teams. Trust was compromised. We had unhappy teams, unhappy sales and product management, and, most important, unhappy customers. This was not exactly a recipe for success.

First things first. I knew I had to somehow find a way to play into the "What is in it for me?" scenario. Looking at this situation from the Quality Integral Map point of view, I could totally see the frustration from all angles. Product management, who controlled the investment for the product team, was upset because despite the cost associated with the team, no releases had gone out for over three years. Product teams were frustrated because they had spent lots of time and effort and right before they were ready to go out with a release they were told there was no market for the features that they had developed. Sales was upset because for a couple of years they'd had nothing new to sell. And customers felt that we were not a thoughtful leader that they wanted to have as a long-term partner. After all, they hadn't seen any innovation from our product team for a few years.

Automation Economics

Considering the landscape, I couldn't play the "newbie" card and go ask for an investment to fix the automation crises without showing specific savings and helping product management understand what the ROI would be for them. So, I got to work! I started to get data on the execution time, quality of test cases, and understanding the level of effort/investment needed to operationalize the semi-complete new headless automation framework.

It was unclear if a thorough review of test cases was done to decide if the entire test suite needed to be executed. Doing a simple analysis of executing even a portion of the entire regression test suite wouldn't allow for good coverage for the release. We needed to keep the current release on track and in parallel do a holistic test-strategy review and sanitize the test cases so everyone on the team (and not just QE) could run them.

I met with the architects and the QE teams and got a high-level feel for what testing was available for different dimensions of testing and for the mapping that was required to execute such tests at different stages of the release. The 12,000+ tests were all in the functional layer. It took some time to create a few categories of tests. We needed to break down the problem to be able to attack it. The team was able to identify and clearly mark all sanity tests that had the highest priority to start off with in our automation journey. We then calculated the time it took one person to execute that small suite of tests and considered the execution frequency for them and came up with a significantly high dollar amount. I then did a similar analysis for the more in-depth tests and calculated the number of hours translated in dollars that it would save if we were to automate such tests. I also emphasized the fact that while such investment is done once, the benefits would be observed throughout the current and future releases.

Once I collected all necessary data I presented it to the product-management leader. I am pretty sure he wasn't paying full attention to what I was presenting until I showed the page that had savings in dollars. Then, he and the rest of the leadership team seemed to wake up and asked me to run through the analysis for them one more time. It was hard to argue with data. Acknowledging that what we had was not scalable and the desire to release more often led to long discussions and finally getting the investment we needed to move forward with the short-and long-term automation plans. I was very excited and pleased with the outcome.

Our quality engineers were out of practice with the automation code writing. We needed to push forward with manual test execution to keep the release in flight, but made an investment for future releases. I got a volunteer from the architecture team to help retrain our engineers. Given the tight schedule we had, we used some of the funding I got to cater lunch and dedicated two hours for lunch three days out of the week for team members and especially our QE members to come together, have lunch, and learn the ins and outs of the new automation framework.

They got a chance to learn, practice, and make a difference. They were exercising muscles that they hadn't used in a while, and they started to like it! The culture was changing. Quality engineers were excited to learn something new and were willing to go beyond. Many were automating test cases on their own time and over the weekends. We started to see automated test numbers going up way earlier than we had anticipated. It was an exciting time. Developers were offering a helping hand, and they too wanted to learn the new framework. No one enjoyed running through test cases manually over and over again and were all motivated to help operationalize the new automation framework.

Long story short, we were able to shave off three weeks from the end of the current release, which was not even accounted for in the plan. When calculated in dollars and considering the number of teams and functions involved in the release, the initial investment had already paid off and more. In addition, we were dealing with a much happier and collaborative team with a common focus and higher hopes for future releases. We also enjoyed the additional quality that was built into the process, even if it was a small percentage of continuous regression tests that were running daily. That effort continued, and the number of automated tests increased for use in future releases.

Addressing Performance-Testing Challenges

Performance (load, scalability, and endurance) testing was a whole other challenge. After reviewing what was being done in the performance group, it became clear that they were working in a silo and that broader guidance was needed from the architects and individual teams for them to even understand what needed to be measured and how. An in-depth analysis was needed to take inventory of what was available and why it would take till the end of the release to assess the performance of the application.

To know where to start and what to do next, we established a tiger team consisting of senior architects who were most familiar with the product and the low-level code, as well as members of our Support department to better understand current customer challenges with regards to the response time and scalability of the older releases of the application. Many customer tickets were analyzed, and a few customers were interviewed to better understand how the product was being used under heavy load. Current test scenarios were updated, performance tools were assessed, and environments were inspected to come up with a starting point. Baselines for simple metrics were created, and a product owner was assigned to the performance scrum team to ensure full understanding of customers' performance expectations for key functionalities.

The global team members started to work together in a scrum team to "follow the sun model" based on clear performance goals set for various operations. That created so much interest within the organization that I started to receive inquiries from senior-level developers to join our performance team. They wanted to help with creating an automated strategy to effectively create a baseline and do a release-over-release and build-over-build performance comparison. That allowed for much more frequent feedback than the model that was in place to run performance assessment only at the end of releases.

Incorporating Customer Input and Use Cases

We had many other areas to focus on. We knew some of our strategic customers had created their own test plans to validate releases before they put them into production. Up until then, we hadn't bothered to learn whether they were running a similar set of test cases or had created a totally different set. It was important to reach out to the account teams and see if we could collaborate with a customer to get their test plans and compare them to our own. The benefit to them would be to reduce their internal investment, and for us it would mean catching issues in our environment before the release, which would translate into fewer support calls. That project also got initiated, and engagement with the first customer got under way.

Another important area was to understand customers' upgrade challenges. Reviewing support cases revealed a very important finding: many upgrades for that product were failing because customers had customized the application in their environment. Once their application was upgraded they would lose all their customizations that they had spent a lot of time to set up. Understanding their challenges better and having access to their data so as to do internal validation for them would make a huge difference.

We started to create programs under the umbrella of "Customer Journey and Engagement." We established three different tracks over time:

- **Tour of our product**

    - This was a program where we met with different customers regularly via WebEx and asked them to walk us through their usage of our application. Those sessions were recorded and played back for our entire QE and development teams.

    - The learnings from those sessions were invaluable. The entire team would use those learnings to enhance the design and testing of certain modules that were used the most, and they tried to enhance automation in those areas as well. After a while, those specific scenarios were fully automated to ensure no regression occurred in those existing functionalities when new releases came out.

- **Dev/Buddy Program**

    - The majority of our engineering department hadn't interacted with customers. Once a month, we invited a customer to either come in person or via WebEx to talk to us about their experience with the product.

- This was a great opportunity for our engineering team to understand customer needs and pain points, and our customers very much appreciated having direct access to the development/testing team to provide their feedback.

- **Upgrade Initiative**

  - We partnered with a few customers to get their data in-house and set up an upgrade test bed to do regular upgrades from their current version to the new version of the product to ensure a smooth transition.

  - This reduced the volume of support calls and created a better upgrade experience for customers.

As we got closer to the end of that release and considered the lack of maturity in continuous integration and DevOps, we decided to add additional oversight to carefully prioritize customer- and internally-reported issues. This involved ensuring every fix got multiple levels of review, and impact analysis was done and approved by the development architect, QE architect, and product manager.

Streamlining Platform Support Matrix (PSM)

Our product had an enormous number of items listed on our platform support matrix. We had created a full scrum team to do nothing but focus on certifying different platforms and versions (i.e., operating systems, data bases, browsers, etc.). Many such platforms were not even in use by customers. One initiative that we launched was to create a cross-functional team with members from sales, support, product management, engineering, and services to review our customer-base configurations and determine the following:

- The most popular configurations used by customers

- List of configurations that created the most number of support tickets from our customers

- Reference architectures that were used by our sales and services team during new sales engagement opportunities

- The most stable configurations with no issues reported internally or by customers

Without any telemetry built into the product, the effort in capturing the preceding data was somewhat manual and extremely painful. But the results that we gained out of that exercise were extremely valuable. We narrowed down hundreds of combinations into less than ten configurations that we were able to set up and create automated test scenarios for, and we let those tests run throughout the release cycle and not just at the end. By doing so, we were able to redirect the focus of that scrum team and have them contribute to developing new features on future releases.

Establishing Regular Service-Pack and Hot-Fix Cadences

Another area that we had challenges with was delivering hot fixes and service packs. Looking at some of those challenges, it became clear that because no new releases had gone out, service packs that were meant to be dedicated to defect fixes only, often included new functionalities as well.

The test process for patches/service packs did not include the full regression-test strategy that existed for major/minor releases. As a result, many quality challenges existed with the service packs. Some one-off hot fixes were not managed well and were provided to customers as a result of escalations that involved many layers of the organization. Unfortunately, such fixes were not always merged into the main branch, and when that customer wanted to upgrade later, their hot fixes would often be lost. You can imagine the frustration reported by such customers.

Also, we didn't have a regular cadence for our service packs. Therefore, every escalation that came in and got the attention of our executive team ended up becoming a high-enough priority to generate a hot fix. That took a lot of cycles from the sustaining team, which needed to focus on releasing service packs on a regular cadence.

Over a period of 12 months, we reorganized and redefined our hot-fix/patch/service-pack processes and regular cadence. Sustaining teams responsible for those functions were invited to self-organize as a scrum team to effectively address customer-reported issues and then release in a regular service-pack cadence. Our sustaining team became an extension of the new development team, and new features were prohibited from being included in hot fixes or service packs. As a result of implementing such new processes, the number of escalations and hot fixes dropped from multiple a week to a handful in a year.

It was important to not only focus on short-term quality-improvement items, but also to create a roadmap for continuously attending to known technical debt and quality-impacting factors over time. The results that the product team achieved from working collaboratively and the energy that was generated in the organization convinced the business leaders that continuous focus on improving quality was needed. They realized that such initiatives were necessary in order to have happier internal teams and achieve much higher customer satisfaction.

With continued support and effort from the entire product team, many metrics such as NPS were significantly improved, which led to additional revenue and customer loyalty.

The team continued to invest in handling technical debt and published specific metrics that highlighted the results of their focus on quality-improvement initiatives:

- Hardening phase reduced by over 80 percent
- Training offered to all on automation code and debugging
- Automation coverage grew to over 65 percent
- Performance results improved by over 300 percent
- Platform support matrix was streamlined by over 400 percent
- One-team culture was created and Agile training offered
- Achieved regular service-pack cadence (once per month)
- Customer satisfaction grew to 9 out of 10

Product Team Example 2

Key focus areas:

- Agile transformation and stronger x-func communication
- Establishing a regular release cadence
- Enhancing focus on test strategy and automation

I joined another organization where they were tasked with taking an existing on-premises product and releasing it in the cloud. The release was well underway when I joined the team. Although no one could articulate why my role was needed immediately in that organization, I later realized that the nature of the issues that they were struggling with were slightly different than what I had experienced in the first example. The team had not met their delivery schedule for a controlled release (i.e., only making it available for a small set of customers) after 18 months of hard work.

Quality Challenges for the Team

There were multiple reasons highlighted for missing the release date:

- The internal SaaS platform team's readiness was not considered in the original planning for the release. They were completely isolated from the product team and had their own roadmap and priorities that didn't necessarily map to those of the product team responsible for releasing software.

- A third-party vendor was hired to do some manual testing, but after their contract ended, many issues surfaced in those so-called tested areas. There was not an easy way to find out the details of the testing done by the vendor other than having a checkmark against test cases indicating they had been executed.

- Very few automated tests existed at the unit or functional levels. They had a record of 15,000+ tests in their multiple spreadsheets. Many had been there for over ten years.

- The SaaS release was intended to surprise the market. Therefore, not a whole lot of in-depth discussions were held with potential customers to fully understand their requirements.

- Performance was viewed as something that each scrum team could address on their own. There was no focus on the overall performance of the product. Timeouts were causing downtime in the SaaS sandbox and needed attention.

- While they were "Agile" and had scrum teams with distributed team members, they each also had an engineering manager that was focused on the delivery of their own team's backlog items.

- Email was used as a substitute for getting the global scrum leadership team together to discuss strategies and key deliverables. Many things were assumed that were never clarified.

- There were hundreds of internally reported defects against the prior on-premises release. Similar issues resurfaced when implemented in the SaaS environment. There were also hundreds of additional high-priority customer-reported issues in the backlog to be addressed. On top of all of that, a securability scan was run, but due to the unfamiliarity of team members with the tool that was used and a lack of training around secure coding, those issues had not been categorized or addressed yet.

- Each team was developing their features in their private branch with no specific plans to rebase or merge along the software development process.

- The mindset of the organization did not include quality.

The first week on the job for me involved meeting with various leaders and architects. Because of the challenges associated with the controlled release attempt, the date for GA had been readjusted and pushed out. Individual teams had taken advantage of the delay and added additional stories to complete for the release that were not part of the original scope; this was done without much discussion at the overall release level. The program manager, who was remote, was extremely frustrated as she was not getting timely updates or full visibility into the latest changes, dependencies, and roadblocks. She explained to me how surprises were showing up almost every day when she spoke with the team. She was not able to get proper attention from the head of the product team or any of the engineering leaders. So, she quit!

While the search for her replacement was going on, I decided to help fill in as much as possible. That provided an opportunity for me to get a better understanding of the release status, challenges, and dependencies. My goal was to work with the team to ensure the second attempt of the release was a success. A lack of documentation forced me to go door-to-door and call people to find basic info such as testing tools, branching strategy, source-code location, code-review process, build process, customer engagement, etc. That was a very difficult and exhausting task!

Leadership Mindset

To my surprise, simple questions such as asking for a pointer to the team's DoD or DoR resulted in lots of emotional emails. The team was so consumed and heads down on getting their specific tasks done that they were forgetting about some basic hygiene that needed to be followed. For example, it was common not to write unit tests and expect black box testing to find all defects in the newly written code.

Here is an example of an update that went to the business-unit leader that I was copied on:

> User stories are almost done except they haven't been validated or QA hasn't been available at all as they are still busy with the previous service pack work. We will mark such stories done for now and once QA is available, we will ask them to do a quick validation.

Another interesting response was when I asked about the performance results:

> Performance Testing is done as per needed basis for each scrum team. I personally believe that in Agile everyone owns quality. Therefore, each scrum team is responsible in ensuring the performance of stories they are working on. We don't have an overall performance focus, which means there is no performance scrum team. Each engineering leader is expected to connect and discuss their performance results with others if needed and plan accordingly. Agile provides a lot of flexibilities as you know!

You can imagine how my blood pressure kept on rising higher and higher as I was listening to such conversations. The problem was much deeper; not only did the team have a rigid waterfall mindset, but they were taking bits and pieces of Agile processes, interpreting them in such a way as to justify their wrong approaches, and even messing up the waterfall implementation that they had been using for many years!

Team Organization and Lack of Mindset

Agile introduction trainings had been completed for some teams, but many leaders were struggling as they were not sure if following that model would allow them to release such a complex product in time. The team structure was such that the entire QA team, with the exception of a few, was in a different geographical location. Product managers were mostly US based, but were not that present.

The product was extremely customizable, and the team was very much insisting on implementing the exact same capabilities and flexibilities that were made available for the on-premises version. Product management had initially asked for less-complex features, but left it pretty much up to the engineering teams to provide feedback on what made most sense to deliver as the SaaS version.

Developers were also distributed, and each had a strong opinion on what features made sense to develop first in the cloud. It was pretty obvious that engineering was in charge of deciding what features to work on. They were the key decision makers, not the product management team! They also were the designers of certain features that had successfully been released and adopted by customers in the on-premises version. So, they were trying to mimic the same thing in a SaaS environment without giving any attention to the unique considerations that were necessary to successfully release in the cloud.

In a conversation with one of the senior engineers around the topic of layered testing and how it was critical to focus on both unit and functional tests, the engineer paused and said:

"Frankly, I think you are making too big of a deal about the need for low-level testing. Product manager or QA can test at the UI level when the entire feature is built and highlight issues then. It makes more sense for development to spend their 'valuable time' designing the features and completing code writing instead of creating unit tests or even automated functional tests."

I was speechless!

I actually validated the last comment and mindset by attending one of the standup meetings and observing how they were being conducted. While they had a scrum master for the team, the product manager had decided to facilitate the meetings herself. There were 18 people on the scrum team! I noticed some would show up ten minutes into the meeting. Others were responding to emails while the standup was in progress. Problem solving was taking place during the standup, and the product manager herself would update the team on the results of her testing and would ask team members to validate and log defects. I had never seen such an implementation of Agile!

Based on various comments and observations, it was very obvious that the product team hadn't internalized the importance of building in quality versus testing it afterward. When a new feature was developed, known defects would stay in the backlog for some time and be ignored with the hope of getting to them during the hardening phase, but sometimes the corresponding story would be marked as complete!

Witnessing how developers were not even writing unit tests or validating their new piece of code before throwing it over to QA or the PM to perform UI-level testing really showed the team's lack of maturity. They would rather deal with a backlog of issues later and get recognized for completing the design of features—without much focus on their usability and full functionality. This was a serious cultural issue that needed to be addressed.

There were other examples that revealed a desperate need for coaching and training on how to manage backlog and do proper estimation and sprint planning. When a team's capacity was highlighted to be 50, planning for 100+ points should have immediately been flagged. Instead, teams didn't even pay attention and kept on going. Or, when sprints were set for two weeks and there were many stories on teams' backlogs with 13+ points, it was almost guaranteed that those stories wouldn't get completed.

The product leader was located in the United States and was not much into details so long as the weekly updates had no red flags listed. I am a firm believer that the culture needs to be adopted at all levels—especially at the leadership level. Getting the leader of the organization to understand the impact of what quality was and how it needed to be adopted across the organization was going to be challenging. Effective communication, transparency, collaboration, and basic Agile and software-development practices were missing with that product team and especially with the leadership team.

Initial Assessment of the Product Team

Once again, I found myself swimming against the flow. Building awareness and changing the culture—starting with the leaders and influential senior engineers—seemed the best way to start the journey. Collecting data and presenting it in the first town hall meeting was my way of testing the waters and learning whether there was even any appetite in the organization to make a change. I shared the summary I had put together based on my initial observations with the business-unit leader first and asked if I could share it in his upcoming town hall. He agreed.

After getting introduced in that first town hall, I shared the set of observations summarized in Figure 4-2 and asked for feedback. Basically, I wanted to know if any of the items also resonated with other members of the team.

List of Challenges Reported by Teams

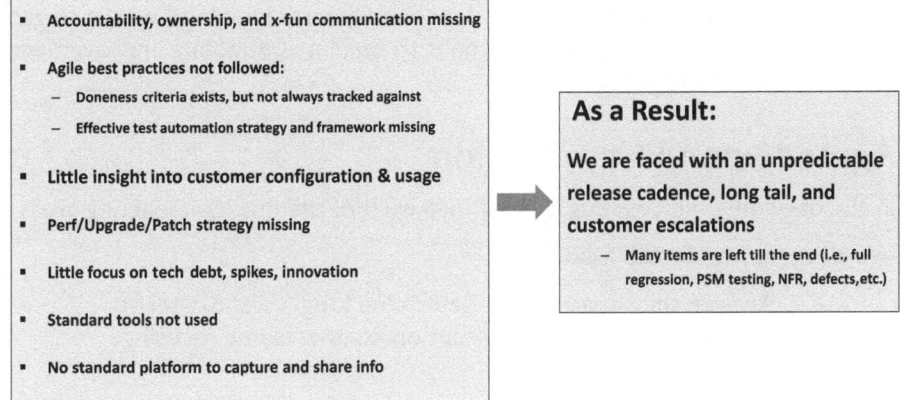

- Accountability, ownership, and x-fun communication missing

- Agile best practices not followed:
  - Doneness criteria exists, but not always tracked against
  - Effective test automation strategy and framework missing

- Little insight into customer configuration & usage

- Perf/Upgrade/Patch strategy missing

- Little focus on tech debt, spikes, innovation

- Standard tools not used

- No standard platform to capture and share info

As a Result:

We are faced with an unpredictable release cadence, long tail, and customer escalations
  - Many items are left till the end (i.e., full regression, PSM testing, NFR, defects,etc.)

Figure 4-2. Initial list of observations that was shared with the entire product team

Something really interesting happened after the town hall. I got bombarded with emails from two separate groups:

- A large group of people who found the summary refreshing, as they too had brought up many similar points without getting any traction from management in the past. They even offered their help to participate in initiatives to help improve the situation!

- A small group of people who seemed to be in denial and were frankly offended to be called an anti-Agile team. But it was hard to present my findings in any other way.

I was encouraged by the feedback and knew that if I could start engaging with the group of people that also realized that changes were needed we could perhaps find a way forward to make a difference. I was very excited to see that the people in this category consisted mostly of senior-ranked engineers, senior product managers, and a couple of engineering leaders.

I invited the group of supporters to the first "Improvement Brainstorming" session. The best time that would get the most participation from key people around the world was at 1:00 a.m. my local time. I took it and held the first meeting, which included follow-ups on the points that I had shared in the town hall. After the two hours that the meeting was scheduled for, it was obvious that team members still had more ideas to share and wanted to discuss further.

Given the fact that everyone was busy with their tasks for the current release, I was very careful not to take too much time away from the entire organization. Instead, I asked for a few volunteers that were most passionate about the necessary changes, and I got more than what I had hoped for. They were so happy about getting visibility into such key success drivers that they offered to capture their thoughts and meet daily for a couple of weeks to get a prioritized list of quality technical debt to build a continuous improvement plan against. I was ecstatic!

Agreed-upon Plan of Action

In the daily meetings, we dug deeper into each of the quality-impacting areas.

We all agreed to do the following:

- Analyze the situation and determine long- vs. short-term solutions to minimize disruption to the teams focusing on the current release.

- Focus on known pain points that impacted productivity and velocity.

- Define a list of necessary improvements, create a roadmap with associated backlog items to deliver against, and publish metrics to track improvements.

- Execute flawlessly and hold each other accountable while providing full transparency; raise the quality bar!

- Do things right the first time and reduce rework.

- Leverage the on-demand logs from regular internal customer feedback and ensure external customers are signed up to have access to early feature development work to provide timely feedback.

- Optimize speed, quality, and productivity:

  - Invest in technical debt now to enjoy increased velocity over time:

    - Automation framework enhancement

    - API as well as UI performance use cases

    - Clean up dead code

- Focus on metrics that are relevant to an SaaS-based product and leverage the data that is readily available to improve internal processes.

- Get trained on Agile and seek help from Agile coaches along the transformation journey.

- Go back to basics on Agile, doneness criteria, training, coaching, learning and leveraging from other scrum teams, and providing tools to be successful.

From the comprehensive list of items to focus on, few short-term solutions were chosen to operationalize first:

- Ensure product management/owner teams are fully engaged with the scrum teams to review stories and help them fully understand the requirements. Having solid acceptance criteria is much needed so as to know when the team is going to be done with their work and eliminate guessing on how the functionality should work.

- All acceptance criteria items are to be met before a story is marked as complete. No open defects are allowed for new stories. Every defect has to be addressed and closed. Basically, statements such as "Everything for this story is done except" are not acceptable and will not be demoed.

- SaaS log access is to be provided to each scrum team to review early feedback from internal and external customers to avoid a big flow of defects late in the process.

- Overall application performance requirements are to be created and the system team are to do the initial baseline in a test sandbox.

The team acknowledged the fact that adding a few quality measures to the release and allowing the manual test execution to proceed for the current release while attending to a longer-term strategy for future releases was the right approach.

The only change in regard to the manual testing was to sprinkle impacted-regression testing into each of the remaining iterations. The assessment of the regression test cases and their categorization was to be put on the priority list of technical debt for right after the release. Overall test strategy needed an overhaul.

Economics View of Quality Continuous Improvement

In parallel, I needed to try to get my business-unit leader on board along with his leadership team. I knew for business leaders ROI would be the best way to get their attention. Collecting data and converting them into dollar amounts that were consumable at that level was going to be my focus. Playing into the worldview of all individuals and functions involved and articulating the financial benefits of quality-focused initiatives were going to once again be my plan of action. You can see why, over time, this approach was referred to as *Navid's Law of Quality Cost Estimation and Benefits!*

The first step was to team up with the product team's senior engineers and the support and services team to get details on the number of calls that came in about product defects, the number of escalations on a weekly basis, the amount of time it took to manually test features, and the number of hours that were spent in very long standups and end-of-sprint demo meetings. This information provided all the necessary financial data that I needed to justify the short-and long-term investments. This effort paved the road for changing the company's mindset and adding investment for continuous quality improvement.

Quality Roadmap

The entire product team created a clear quality roadmap to keep focus on short-term, mid-term, and longer-term quality initiatives. For example, they agreed that soon after the current release, there was a dire need to focus on building a new automation framework and then assess test cases with assigned priorities to be automated. The following is part of a plan that the leadership team agreed to after many hours of review and discussion:

- Refresher course in Agile was to be provided immediately after the current release.

- Assigned one architect to API-based and one to UI-based automation initiatives.

  - Reviewed framework, audit scripts, and mentor teams and ensured highest-priority test cases were automated.

- One hour per QA per day per team (including sustaining) for test-case assessment and cleanup was needed; instruction was provided.

  - Phase 1 just to identify test cases that required modification/repair or were duplicates or obsolete.

  - Phase 2 to add missing steps and clean up test cases marked to be repaired.

- Starting in the following release, all scrum teams had to meet their new feature test-case automation goal, no exceptions. The entire scrum team was responsible, not just QA.

- Needed a local scrum master for this effort to monitor daily progress and publish metrics.

The product team also agreed on the following areas to better engage customers:

- Invited customers to give us a tour of how they used our product.
  - PM took this action item to help with identifying interested customers to engage with engineering.
  - Learned their pain points and focused engineering effort there.
  - Created a heat map of internal and customer-reported issues to decide on popularly utilized modules.
- Established a regular internal voice of the customer feedback gathering.
  - Provided updated servers at the end of each sprint to all internal customers (i.e., presales, support, education, services, etc.).
- Performed SaaS log analysis for usage of various modules and work flow by customers.

Also, we established a set of story doneness criteria as follows to deliver against:

- User Story Doneness
  - Acceptance criteria met and test cases reviewed
  - Code complete, code reviewed, and unit tested (all unit tests automated)
  - All automatable functional test cases automated
  - Regression tested per impacted areas (no new bugs introduced)
  - All planned test cases executed, passed, and results published
    - Included all relevant abilities per iteration (i.e., I18n, securability,…)
  - All bugs (Sev 1, 2, 3, 4) addressed (triaged, resolved [could include "will not fix"] and validated)
  - Tech documentation updated
  - Wiki, test-case management tool, and defect- and story-monitoring tools updated
  - Relevant performance use cases created and proper load tests successfully run

We also stated that if the preceding criteria were not met, there was not going to be a demo!

The preceding statement regarding not being allowed to showcase your work if you hadn't met all the listed Definition of Done items, initially created some anxiety among teams. I got a note from one of the engineering leaders saying that preventing teams from showcasing their work after working so hard to have working software was against Agile. So what, if the testing is not done yet. The software works for the most part. My response was, the "most part" is not highlighted in Agile; in fact, there is a lot of emphasis on the Definition of Done for all work in Agile that you seem to be ignoring.

I am pleased to say that over time, the majority understood the importance of following a solid DoD and DoR and started to comply with it and actually enjoyed the results. Some who didn't cope with the required changes unfortunately left the organization, which was expected.

Once again, for this product team we needed to focus on the release in flight to ensure it got wrapped up as per some level of agreement with various cross-functional team members, such as product management, sales, engineering, SaaS platform hosting teams, support, and services. In the meantime, it was critical to capture a prioritized list of required quality-improvement items in the product backlog to address in future releases. With the overwhelming number of quality items that needed attention, the prioritization was key to ensure every team was committed to setting aside bandwidth in every iteration to attend to such critical items as per the agreed-upon priority. It was important to continuously remind the teams that such items had been ignored for many years and that expecting to get through them all immediately was not possible. That is why it is referred to as the quality-improvement journey!

Fast forward to two years from that time:

- Cross-functional engagement at all levels of the development cycle allowed for better planning and prevented surprises at the end.

- A functional scrum-team model was put in place with co-located teams and a single backlog for the entire organization to follow.

- All scrum teams were guided and coached through the adoption of Agile quality methods, enhanced automation, and increased collaboration.

- Regular service-pack cadence and major/minor release model prevented the need for regular hot fixes.

- These improvements led to a nearly 50 percent reduction in operating expenses in less than two years and over $2.5M in automation-driven efficiency.

We had happier business leaders, customers, and scrum-team members!

Business Unit Example 3

The key focus was on:

- Creating a culture of quality across the business unit.
- Going back to basics on Agile processes and adopting common standards.
- Reducing the number of escalations.
- Improving NPS.

An opportunity showed up for me to be a quality consultant in a large organization with ten product teams. This came right after a long and difficult transformation journey at my previous job. A logical approach most people would take after such a long and difficult journey would be to stay put and enjoy, relax, and witness the success of the team that had worked so hard to get to a much higher quality maturity level by following Agile disciplines. But the new opportunity was tempting!

When I spoke with the general manager for the new organization, I found out about many quality challenges, including, but not limited to

- routine escalations by unhappy customers;
- employee-retention challenges due to recent organizational changes that had been made prior to his leadership;
- lack of a solid DevOps practice;
- lack of predictability on releases; and
- lots of unhealthy tension between various functions in the organization.

It all sounded like a great opportunity to make a difference. That is at least how I looked at it!

If you have ever walked into an organization where, by asking a simple question of "How is it going?" you get a lot more information than you can process, then you know exactly what I experienced during my first few days on the job. I joined an organization that needed so much focus on various aspects of quality (including educating the leadership team) that I was overwhelmed as to where to begin. That is when meditation and yoga really would have come in handy! Every person that I spoke with in private shared a new set of challenges that were not being discussed as a team. That, to me, was a sign of a lack of trust and transparency!

During my first week on the job, I was invited to four customer-escalation calls. They were similar in nature. The customer was extremely unhappy about a problem that had impacted their production or a functionality that they had been using that suddenly had stopped working after their recent upgrade.

Since I was hired to lead quality in that organization, the same comment was made after every call/meeting: "Navid, now you can see why we desperately need help in QA. Many of these calls could have been prevented if QA had caught the issues internally." After the second time I heard that comment, I couldn't take it anymore and started to highlight the fact that with the complex nature of any product, there was no way that QA could test every possible scenario and report all issues. I had to go back to basics with the team and remind them that defect prevention is much more effective than testing and looking for defects after the code is complete. We discussed some basic software-development hygiene and the fact that quality is the responsibility of the entire organization and not just QA. Quality needs to be built into the product and not bolted on after it is released!

A Peek into the Current Landscape

During the first few days of working with a couple of team members, I was able to collect some insight into the current state of challenges. The following examples seemed to be directly impacting customer quality:

- While claiming to be Agile, many disciplines were not internalized.
  - Team collaboration was not common; division of responsibilities even among the same scrum team negatively impacted the progress.
  - There was no focus on Severity 3 and 4 issues, even in newly developed features.
- Fixed date and expanded scope!
  - It was not uncommon to see new requirements from product management in the middle of a sprint.
  - The expectation was of course to still meet the set GA date even after the additional requested updates and changes were added to the scope.
- Performance and other "abilities" were left for hardening.
  - A performance-testing plan existed in pockets but was not followed consistently.
  - There were no requirements around scalability and longevity, which many customers were asking for.
  - There was a plan to do performance testing late in the release cycle and during hardening. This had been the practice in the past, and I was told at times that when complex performance issues were unveiled during hardening teams were pressured to ship despite known issues just to keep on schedule.

- Supportability was not considered. Engineering had to be pulled into many customer calls since diagnostability was not built into the application.

- A very large platform support matrix was common across the business unit.

  - Backward compatibility with prior versions and platforms was a major challenge.

- The automation framework was very unstable.

  - The results were intermittent at best.

  - The framework was not very user friendly and not very popular with developers. Therefore, they were not motivated to spend much time resolving issues.

- There was no test strategy that was being followed for the business unit as a whole.

  - Full regression was planned for the hardening phase.

  - No concept of impacted regression testing for new stories existed.

  - Thousands of test cases were in the regression test suite but had no priority assigned to them. They were left to the QA engineers to decide what tests to run and when.

- They hadn't released a quality software for over two years.

  - Since a few enhancements were needed to stay competitive, it was not uncommon to ship service packs that included new functionalities.

- There were frustrated team members and unhappy customers.

  - Morale was extremely low, and retention of high performers was a major issue.

  - Customers were unhappy, and escalations were coming in at a very high weekly rate for all product lines.

I knew there were more items on the list that I would learn about in more detail after getting to know the teams and various products.

Getting to Know the Teams, Key Players, and Challenges Better!

After a couple of weeks on the job, I was asked to attend a cross-functional meeting with leaders and senior architects/engineers on the East Coast. This was the first time that product-team representatives from different geographical locations were coming together. There was a two-day meeting scheduled to discuss objectives for the year and common challenges. The meetings were great for a new person like myself to get to know different players and learn about their products and quality challenges. The organization had invested in Agile and SAFe training and had decided that all members of scrum teams needed to help with development and testing. Since developers could perform both functions of developing code and testing it, a decision had been made by the prior leader of the organization to save money by laying off more than 90 percent of all QA engineers. On one major product team, they had let go of all but one senior QA! One of the key discussion points in the two-day meeting was how to ensure success despite changes and clarify risks associated with such decisions.

It was an interesting meeting, to say the least. I took some notes and summarized my findings to send the following email to my boss (the general manager):

I am on my way back home and wanted to take this opportunity to provide my thoughts on what I observed during the week. Obviously, I need to validate some of my understandings. But for now, here is my view of the organization in various categories:

Leadership:

- *I found most of the leaders to be focused on tactical items without any specific strategy or vision. Some are technical and at the same time have very little leadership and management skills.*

- *The division of responsibilities among the product teams in the United States versus other locations did not make much sense to me.*

- *Teams are working in silos, and that is alarming. Also, the role of a site leader in various locations is a bit confusing, even to other leaders that I spoke with.*

- *Elevating teams doesn't seem to be a priority. Not much is being done to leverage skillsets and focus on strengths of individuals.*

- *Innovation in everything that teams do is not emphasized much, and innovation is being seen mostly in the context of patents.*

- *There is no deep understanding of Agile/SAFe. Mindset is still waterfall in most teams.*

- *There seem to be transparency issues that lead to not sharing true strengths and weaknesses.*

- *Spoke with the only lead quality engineer on one of the product teams, and he was extremely relieved that I was freely talking about the importance of quality practices. Apparently, that is not the culture today.*

- *He told me that we got rid of his entire QA team, and many were picked up by our customers or competition due to their deep level of product knowledge. Retaining what is left of our QA talent should be made a priority as such engineers are unsure about their future in this organization.*

Technical Skillset:

- *There are some major skillset mismatches or simply missing skills, such as performance/DBA/basic software development 101 (i.e., code reviews, unit tests, automation strategy) and, most important, product knowledge.*

- *I couldn't get a straight answer on how many people today have some sort of certification that supports the domain knowledge required to work on the complex product lines in the organization.*

- *Most QAs that were let go had a deep overall product knowledge and that is now missing and is a major contributing factor to code quality and much frustration on the teams.*

- *The architect team is not deeply engaged with the challenges that the product teams are faced with. Their backlog seems to consist of cool future technology items that don't align with the roadmap for the teams. Some architects don't seem to have key skills necessary to guide the rest of the technical teams, which defeats the purpose of having architects around. After talking to a couple of the architects, it felt that they didn't know what their responsibilities were as an architect!*

Collaboration:

- *Due to the division of responsibilities and volume of work, there is very little knowledge sharing that takes place.*

- *Cross-pollination is not common or encouraged.*

- *I found out that sustaining and core teams are not even comparing notes (i.e., hundreds of tests are run on every service pack on one product without any correlation/feedback to what is executed on major/minor releases for that same product).*

- *There is no common forum for development and testing folks to share strategy and best practices. Some don't even know key engineers in other global locations to collaborate with. Everyone is heads down focusing on their own tasks and fearful to speak up if they need additional help.*

- *There is no Agile coach to help guide the teams.*

Customer Engagement and Focus:

- *Forward-development teams seem to be working in isolation and do not have much visibility into customer pain points. Issues from support that come in often go back and forth multiple times before they get resolved. Meeting with support counterparts to discuss ticket priority is not part of the culture. Frustration and disconnect exist on both sides of the aisle.*

- *In one of the breakout sessions, I shared how lagging indicators (i.e., tracking the number of customer defects in each of the component areas, emergency fixes, MTTR, etc.) along with customer-like scenarios would bring better visibility on what customers value. Everyone was supportive of introducing such metrics and publishing them on a regular basis, but I was surprised that it wasn't thought about till now.*

- *I talked to the head of product management about bringing the customer voice into the organization. He didn't think getting a few customers lined up to meet on a monthly basis would be an issue. Until that becomes a reality, I met with the head of support to organize regular support/engineering meetups to discuss monthly hot spots for customer. Getting support and services engaged with the development teams to share regular feedback on the state of various releases in production is key. Also, sharing specific utilities that they develop to resolve customer issues would be a significant first step in getting a quality mindset in the development department.*

- *A rotation program for developers and support engineers is always a great learning tool as well. It will provide insight for the development team on what customers care about and what can be done to deliver better value to them.*

Tools and Automation:

- *Every team seems to have a different set of tools, technologies, and approaches to solve customer issues.*

- *I am unclear about the overall automation strategy. There seems to be a lot of different approaches and toolsets that teams use, but I am not convinced they are the right tools or they are even providing the expected ROI (i.e., I learned that after spending many months to develop and implement a new automation framework, some team members were not convinced that it was the best framework. They had decided to start another initiative to investigate a different framework. When I asked detailed questions regarding the requirements for the framework, no one seemed to have a list of specific requirements based on which they had made the decision to develop the prior framework or for selecting the best automation framework going forward).*

  - *For automation in particular, we really need a senior developer/architect to help evaluate if the toolsets and framework used are the best match for our tech stack. They first need to develop a set of requirements.*

  - *Lots of focus seems to have been put on investigations that didn't amount to anything practical.*

- *Accessing quality data is challenging. There seems to be a lot of tribal knowledge that is not written down and usually resides with one individual—a huge risk.*

Here is a short list of immediate actions that can be done to avoid building further quality technical debt. It will be time consuming, but we have to start at some level. In talking to a couple of leaders and digging deeper into some known issues, they found spending time in the following areas to be valuable:

Short-Term Approaches:

- *Assess skillsets for the team members and create a learning matrix.*

- *Build the product knowledge that was lost with removing QA engineers to help with reducing the hardening phase.*

- *Promote basic software-development practices (i.e., code reviews, peer programming, etc.).*

- *Finalize our automation strategy and tools (may require consulting budget).*

- *Identify key standards, templates, and metrics to educate and promote transparency.*

- *Prioritize list of relevant test cases in test repository.*

- *Establish a must-have list of DoD and DoR and ensure teams follow.*

Long-Term Approaches:

- *Create a quality-improvement roadmap and ensure inclusion of quality-impacting items on the product backlog for continuous improvement. Some examples are:*

  - *Engage with customer-facing organizations to understand customers' pain points better.*

  - *Perform value-stream analysis to improve CI/CD.*

  - *Implement an effective automation framework.*

  - *Create accountability around Agile practices (i.e., DoD/ DoR, retro, effective demos, etc.).*

  - *Understand performance requirements and create a framework.*

  - *Streamline platform support matrix (PSM).*

  - *Establish a common system test approach.*

  - *Conduct regular release review sessions to get visibility into the release progress as well as the team's focus on ongoing quality improvement.*

As you can see, opportunities were abundant! Where to start was the real million-dollar question: *Where to begin?*

The role of a quality consultant was a new one for the business unit and did not exist previously. So, inserting myself in the right forum and meetings and creating a safe environment and trust among team members was my initial goal. My objective was to be accepted as part of the team and not be viewed as a cop or an auditor. Convincing a few leaders in the organization of the need to change was the first step toward getting focus on quality-related initiatives. Also, having our GM highlight the importance of this element helped in getting the right level of focus from the organization.

In the first town hall meeting, the GM introduced me as the new quality leader who would partner with the teams to help bring focus on quality. This intro was followed by stating that "Driving Focus on Quality and Execution" was now going to be the number one strategy for the entire organization in that fiscal year!

That left no doubt in people's minds that we were serious about focusing on quality. They needed more clarification on what quality meant and how it was going to get the right level of attention when there were so many other priorities. Everyone knew that the current situation was not scalable, with delayed releases and daily customer escalations. Team members were hungry for change and needed a strong strategy to help support it.

The Call to Action from the leadership team around quality was as follows:

- Product teams – Focus your backlog to drive the realization of our strategy.
  - Continue to drive your efforts in quality:
    - Value to customers
    - Velocity – time to value
    - Total cost of ownership
  - Continue to drive the business forward with new and growing sales opportunities.
  - Stay responsive to the customer-facing teams (sales, support, and services).

It was also mentioned that going forward, an update on quality-focused initiatives was to be highlighted in quarterly town hall meetings. This was a very powerful message and the one that it was important to draw the entire organization's attention to. After all, no one wanted to be showcased as a team with no focus on quality when it was specifically communicated as the number one strategy for the entire business unit.

The strong message around quality and putting customers at the front and center really helped me begin my journey in the organization. I needed to get to know the triads (dev architect, PM, engineering leader) and key influencers for each product team. Meeting with as many functions and individuals as time permitted to provide a clear picture of what challenges existed in each product team was necessary to come up with priorities for the organization. Maturity levels were different for each product team. While a common quality framework was needed to work off of for the entire business unit, we needed to work at a much lower level on one product team to show value and validate with a proof of concept.

The PMO (Program Management Office) team in that organization had trained the leaders in Agile and SAFe. However, just like many other departments, they were focusing more on the process and mechanics of Agile than on the outcome that they needed to achieve. In one of my early trips to meet one of the product teams, I was told that the team had gained a lot of speed since transitioning into Agile. When they were asked about their challenges, it was highlighted that striking the right balance between releasing on time and meeting quality requirements was an area that always brought tension to the team. At times, they were forced to make a decision to ship when features were not fully baked, validated by any customers, or even had known high-priority defects. While those messages were painful to hear, I was happy that teams were feeling comfortable to share them with me and speak up.

Regular Cross-Functional Engagements Helped Zoom in on Quality Priorities

I and other product team members attended many escalation calls with unhappy customers that really helped guide our focus on quality. Pulling teams away on a regular basis to put out fires was not scalable. We needed a better solution, and we needed it fast! Another great source of info was engaging with the customer-facing organizations. It was surprising to me that the members of the development team didn't even know who the support engineers on their product were. Asking them to review volume-driver analysis provided by support was a foreign concept to them. The head of support compiled a list of hot spots for each product as well as other key metrics such as MTTR along with customer satisfaction scores on a monthly basis. All engineering and product-management leaders were in attendance, but they still needed a focused plan to take action.

Regular engagement with members of support, SWAT, services, product management, and presales provided invaluable information to help guide us on what mattered to the customers and what needed to be the highest priority for the product teams. It was refreshing to see the excitement and offers to help with initiatives to help improve product quality. I was asked to attend customer calls with sales so they could highlight the importance of quality at our business unit. Having a quality leader that sat on the GM's staff to be the customer's advocate and focus on quality resonated positively with the customers. It showed that quality had a seat at the table!

One great resource to help focus our attention on the highest-impacting quality factors was the analysis that our SWAT team had done on the total cost of ownership for various products. That analysis resulted in a clear picture of what areas were costing the company (and our customers) the most and needed immediate attention. Even starting with one item and building our backlog over time would help extensively. That spreadsheet had details regarding various categories of issues reported by customers and feedback from certain customers on what would be considered the most value add for future releases. Deployment cost and delivering value on time needed to get attention first and were highlighted as the highest-contributing cost factors.

That seemed like a great starting point on which to do value-stream analysis so as to learn what specific factors product teams could focus on to help resolve such challenges. Getting information from cross-functional team members also helped clarify what needed to be prioritized in the backlog to address quality challenges and show continuous improvement.

Once again, I realized that while quality was considered as being important to our customers, dedicating budget to investing in quality-improvement initiatives had not been considered. Going back to the Worldview concept and Quality Integral Theory and emphasizing the expected business value as a result of focusing on key quality-improvement factors was the approach we took here as well.

Economics of Focusing on Quality-Improvement Journey

We totally understood that sales couldn't add "higher quality" as a new feature to compete with other vendors. However, we could improve product quality to deliver easier-to-use higher value to customers and reduce expenses associated with the support calls. The tangible (reducing support calls) and intangible (higher customer satisfaction) savings could be invested in ongoing quality improvements. Funding our own objectives by showing cost savings was the approach we needed to take.

After attending a release-team meeting for one of the products, I realized that they were struggling with how to prioritize quality-impacting features (or technical debt items) against features to deliver new functionality. The approach that the team was taking to prioritize backlog items was based on a lean method that considered current business context, value, risk, and effort. It was hard to come up with a tangible weighted factor for quality items.

One simple ROI analysis for one product team where a lack of automation had forced them to involve the entire organization to manually test the product helped secure a separate budget to hire an external automation vendor. It was important to make sure the budget was spent wisely to show the expected ROI. Given the team's prior unfavorable experience with third-party automation vendors, we decided to manage a new vendor as if they were our own team members:

- Ensured the automation framework was documented well to be consumed by internal and the third-party vendor.

- Third-party team members were asked to reside on site and work with the internal team.

- Internal senior engineers were asked to provide training and do code reviews to ensure once the project was done internal team was well versed in maintaining automated tests.

- The vendor was held to the same standards as the internal Agile teams with daily standups and updates, demos, and transparency on blocking issues.

Influencing the culture after many years of teams' focusing on releasing new features with little emphasis on quality was challenging. Few new leaders were hired into the organization and had participated in successful transformations elsewhere. At least they understood the objectives and were providing their full support to move forward with such initiatives. Also, the willingness for customer-facing departments to help support such quality-improvement initiatives really helped our cause. Our support department had already started to focus on the customer journey. They had analyzed great opportunities to retain customers and build loyalty with our customer base—but only if we could keep product quality at a high level.

It took a good few weeks to capture all feedback, understand what initiatives were already underway, create excitement about the strategic priorities, and identify departments and individuals that could significantly contribute to this initiative. It was important to emphasize to the teams that quality had not been a priority for the company in the past. However, with the new leadership team and clear objectives, we now had an opportunity to change and listen to our customers.

Focusing on Agile Practices Was a Key Ingredient to Influence Quality

Skillsets and roles of individuals in the Agile world seemed to be confusing to many. Even with the architect council, it was unclear what their priorities were. They were distant from the scrum teams and were working on cool technologies that were not on any of the team's backlogs. That was a major disconnect and a great opportunity to leverage skillsets. Some scrum teams were operating without the help from a product owner or a scrum master. System teams were unclear on their objectives. Anything that scrum teams didn't want to tackle (integration, upgrade, installation, and build challenges) were passed on to that team. There was no product owner assigned, and the engineering managers for those system teams were working off of a backlog that was not in alignment with the scrum team's delivery schedule.

Characteristics of an Architect

A great architect in another business unit had scheduled a webinar on the role of an architect. I sent a recording link of that session to all of our architects and asked that everyone review the recording. That generated a lot of great discussions and helped bring some architects closer to the teams. Here were few items highlighted for the architects in that webinar:

- Understand the business domain.

- Focus on the architectural runway; include technical debt.

- Guide teams on standard software-development processes.

- Be flexible on scope but don't compromise quality.
- Simplify essential complexity and articulate value to teams.
- Be a great listener and be decisive when faced with relevant options as there is no one-size-fits-all solution.
- Must be hands on but not controlling.
- Lead by example and take responsibility for your decision.
- Consider all tradeoffs.
- Focus on common APIs, boundaries, and interfaces.
- Consider the entire abilities space (performance, supportability and maintenance, scalability, installability, upgradability, securability, usability).
- Fully understand the impact of change.
- Help teams look for deficiencies and waste.
- Don't work in isolation.
- System thinking is important and can help reduce TCO.
- Encourage teams to follow meaningful Agile practices.

This was a bit different than what some architects had in mind. They wanted to work on "cool" items that were interesting to them. A few such individuals couldn't perform in the new collaborative environment and left the organization, which is understandable in any transformation. At some point, people either have to get on board or get off the bus!

Clarifying the Path Forward for the Organization

Summarizing what I had heard and where we wanted to get to was important to help communicate not only among the product teams, but also with the customer-facing departments. Simple goal, problem, and strategy statements helped focus the entire organization on what we all needed to expect in the future:

- **Goal**: Deliver high-quality releases on a regular cadence to solve customer problems and be a leader in the industry.
- **Problem Statement**: Product development standard practices and good hygiene have not been a priority in certain areas; as a result, we are faced with challenges that impact product quality and value to our customers in our Agile transformation journey.

- **Strategy**: Enforce modern product development best practices (i.e., architecture, processes, etc.) moving forward and reshape our product backlog to include quality technical debt and achieve our goal.

For every product, the triads were given the task of creating a SWOT analysis. Here is an example of one product team's analysis that helped pave the road for their future success:

Strengths:

- Competitive features and ahead of its time
- Highly customizable and configurable and with a rich feature set
- A tenured team with strong domain knowledge
- Co-located teams

Weaknesses:

- Complex business logic and fragmented validation
- Not a strong quality focus
- Support for too many environments and items on the platform support matrix (PSM) hurting velocity
- Customers on multiple releases and versions that expected full support
- Not good at deprecating unpopular functionalities

Opportunities:

- REST APIs to offer interoperability
- Modern UI
- Invest in automation to reduce hardening phase
- Zero downtime for the SaaS-based version
- Leveraging telemetry to understand customer usage and needs
- Practice Agile at scale

Threats:

- Deficient customer experience
- Deficient in CI/CD and overall test strategy
- Deficient performance and scalability strategy
- Upgrade process is perceived to be error prone

Double-clicking and going deeper in each of the areas and asking the "Five WHY" questions led to better understanding of what needed to be done for each product team. For example, in the area of investing in automation, one product team zoomed in on the following three specific areas. They identified the problem and asked why the problem existed. If the answer did not reveal the root cause, they kept on asking why again until they reached a root cause that they could address.

Automation Framework:

- Current framework is homegrown and intermittent.

- Support for current framework is challenging since original designers are no longer with the company.

- Results are intermittent.

- Need to invest in an open source automation framework, especially with new focus on REST APIs.

Test-case Cleanup:

- Large number of test suites makes it difficult to pick and choose relevant ones.

- Dedicating time to clean up test cases in every iteration is needed.

Training:

- Once a new framework is created, train all members, not just QA,

- Report on test-case automation in every iteration.

With the availability of the SWOT analysis, it became clear that the holistic view of quality needed to be focused on to capture common themes and create pillars that would give teams a clear roadmap of the quality journey. Keeping the momentum going and creating a platform to establish a quality-improvement roadmap and report on progress would help the entire organization to stay focused on key strategic initiatives.

Quality Is Not a Destination, but a Journey

Understanding that quality improvement is not a destination but rather an ongoing journey is very critical for transforming the organization. I was once asked by one of the executive leaders of an organization, "When will we be done with this 'quality stuff?'" I had to swallow, take a deep breath, and respond by saying, "This is not 'stuff'; we need to stay on top of quality-impacting items to continuously improve and be competitive in the market. Customers expect good quality. In fact, they expect to have a culture where quality is given and is built into every step that we take." Obviously, I didn't make a friend that day, but it was important to correct the misunderstanding.

Focus on Influencers, Identify Detractors, and Use Data to Support Initiatives

There will always be people in an organization that will take a while to get on board with major initiatives that involve changes in the mindset and processes that have been around for many years. Sadly, as we saw earlier, some may not ever get on board and will leave the organization. It is important to identify who the key influencers are and ensure they get on board first and convince others to join the movement. Identifying the detractors is just as important because if you don't manage the situation they may derail the initiative. Keep in mind that having data and customer testimonials will be strong tools to help shift people's mindset and get them on board faster. In this particular organization, solid data on total cost of ownership and feedback from our customers spoke for itself and made it much easier to win people over and allow them to get to the conclusion that quality needed a strong seat at the table.

Importance of a Product-Review Process

After getting product teams aligned with the quality-improvement strategy, we also started a Product Review Board across the organization. The product manager, architect, engineering lead, quality lead, and business-unit leader attended the product review sessions. The objective of these quarterly meetings was to assess the health of the current release and understand roadblocks and progress against their quality-improvement roadmap. This allowed for better visibility, transparency, and commitment across the entire business unit. It was also a great opportunity for teams to articulate their challenges, showcase their success, and reduce late-breaking surprises!

The organization did an outstanding job of keeping their focus on quality initiatives, and as a result, within the first 12 months they achieved the following amazing results:

- Quality-related initiatives gained attention across the business unit.

- Agile practices were integrated in the release process and continuously improved upon.

- Escalations reduced from weekly to a handful a year.

- NPS improved by an average of 100 percent across all products.

In this chapter, you have seen references to individual product teams and a business unit that embarked on an Agile quality journey and were able to enjoy significant quality-improvement results. Such outcomes resonated with their customers and, over time, improved their business outcomes as well. The approaches they took and lessons they learned along the way can be mapped to other similar situations.

In the next chapter, we will focus on a solid Agile quality framework to aid teams in creating a blueprint while going through their Agile journey. That will allow teams to have a long-term strategy around quality initiatives and be able to make progress in an ongoing basis.

Self-Reflection Questions

- What challenges do you see in your organization that are similar to the ones listed in the three specific examples in this chapter?

- Why is the role of an architect critical in a quality-transformation journey?

- How did SWOT analysis help focus the team in Example 3?

- Can you identify unique differences between the first two examples that were at the team level versus the third one that spanned across the entire business unit?

- Why is it important for a quality advocate to have a seat at the table?

- Highlight what different steps you would have taken given the specific situations in each of the examples.

- Why is good software-development hygiene important to establish a culture of quality?

- Why is supportability an important "ability" impacting overall quality?

- Why would a team's skillset play a role in the overall product quality?

- Consider a business-impacting factor in your organization.

  - What initiative can you recommend to help remediate the problem?

  - What kind of ROI analysis would you do to convince business leaders to get funding for the initiative?

  - How much money will this initiative save?

Quality Framework

The Five Pillars of Quality

This chapter will focus on how learnings from the individual team experiences were used to create a blueprint and a strong framework for every team across business units to use. Having a solid framework will help elevate the importance of focusing on quality across the board.

After reviewing the SWOT analysis that was carefully crafted by the triads and key decision makers in each of the teams, we noticed a great desire to make a change across the board. There were a few common challenges that needed proper quality investment, such as the long tail end of the release, silos in development and sustaining, lack of a strong test strategy, and a few other factors.

To better understand such challenges and create a strong framework to address these common issues across the organization, we decided to conduct a survey. Over 95 percent of the organization participated in the Agile quality survey. Questions covered their opinions about the health of their own individual scrum team, the overall release team, and their leadership team. In addition, questions regarding specific quality-impacting factors that were preventing them from doing the right thing and doing things right were included in the survey.

© CA 2019
N. Nader-Rezvani, *An Executive's Guide to Software Quality in an Agile Organization*,
https://doi.org/10.1007/978-1-4842-3751-9_5

I took time to read through all the feedback, considered the SWOT analysis by various teams, and categorized responses. In doing so, and in conducting follow-up interviews with various individuals in the organization, it became clear that the quality challenges could be summarized by five quality "pillars." I started to refer to them as Navid's Quality Pillars (NQPs).

The five NQPs were defined as:

1. Team Development and Agile Practices
2. Code Quality and Architecture
3. Agile Productivity and Quality Enablers
4. Abilities
5. Customer Success

Pillar 1: Team Development and Agile Practices

The survey results showed that employees were concerned about the following:

- Multiple reorganizations
- Attrition rate
- Career path
- Lack of true Agile implementation
- Lack of transparency and trust, and a fear of speaking up

Building trust and creating a culture of transparency take a long time. Creating a safe environment where ideas are freely shared and transparency is encouraged is a cultural change that needs to start from the top.

When there is attrition in an organization at all levels, and especially at the leadership level, a very unhealthy environment is formed where team members are in an unclear and confused state. Unless a strong vision is shared and a clear path forward is presented to the teams, building trust among teams will be difficult. Usually, when there is a lot of turnover in an organization, the volume of work doesn't change, and for a while there will be fewer people to get the tasks done. It is even more disturbing when unique skills leave the organization that are not easily replaceable.

In a software company, the key asset is people. After all, you can't have superior software without a superior team! Focusing on growing and attracting new talent, creating a culture of learning, and elevating teams will be key to your company's success. Sometimes it is essential to provide training and proper education so your employees not only learn new things, but also unlearn what was learned previously that may no longer be applicable. This is what I normally refer to as the *Law of Continuous Learning (and Unlearning!)*.

Agile practices and principles are usually taught in a workshop and during training sessions, especially when a large organization is involved. There is not a lot of time to dig through specific real-world examples. So, while the mechanics might be familiar to the team members, unless they practice and get coached along the way, bad behaviors may be promoted.

In many organizations, deficiencies in scrum-team staffing hinder progress and are considered key roadblocks. As an example, some Agile teams operate without an assigned product owner or scrum master. Those two roles are critical in Agile. If a product owner is not available to clarify ambiguities in requirements and answer questions in a timely manner, engineering team members will step in and make a call that may not be in alignment with what customers are looking for.

A similar challenge exists with a shared scrum master role. Teams will struggle with how to best resolve dependencies if they cannot rely on their scrum master. Valuable time will be lost by the scrum team if trained scrum masters are not assigned to specific teams.

When teams are short handed and milestones are fast approaching, it is difficult to consider investing time in learning new skills or tools, or in getting a refresher on basic software development hygiene. In observing the practices followed by several teams, I learned that code would often get checked into the developers branch without any code reviews, or, even worse, because of the lack of time, code review was considered a formality to allow check-ins to proceed. No one really reviewed code, especially if it was written by a more senior individual on the team!

The observations and feedback from team members were invaluable and scary at the same time. We needed to stop the bleeding, and we needed to do it fast. There were a couple of product teams that had been practicing true Agile and had internalized it, but because the rest of the organization hadn't adopted it fully, it was having an impact on their product delivery. Cross-pollination and learning across product teams are usually not common approaches. Even if they cross someone's mind, there is usually no time to invest in learning!

Retaining and attracting talent to build a world-class product organization is often talked about at all levels, and even in some town halls put on by the executives. The same holds true about emphasizing the importance of following proper Agile practices if an organization is expected to go through a transformation. But for it to be effective, the entire organization needs to make the shift, and not just Development and QA.

It is important to ensure that the leadership team is on board with the need to elevate their team, provide training, and ensure proper skills exist in the organization. That usually allows for proper levels of investment to be dedicated to such initiatives. A clear feature can then be created with specific objectives and success criteria to ensure progress is being made.

Example of a Feature to Track Against the First Pillar of Quality

As a leader for the organization, I want to retain and attract talent to build a world-class organization.

Success criteria are:

- *Assess current talent pool in the organization and identify critical gaps to fill:*

  - *Agile Roles*

  - *Technical Skills*

- *Publish a roadmap for training individuals and ensure a story related to the required investment in training is included and prioritized in the product backlog*

Figure 5-1 summarizes the first Navid's Pillar of Quality.

1. Team Development, standard Code Dev & Agile Practices	

Grow talent and adhere to software development practices in an Agile world
 	
Agile is a team sport!
	• Emphasize Product Development Standard Practices
	  • Inclusive to all members of the Prod Team
	  • Build standard software development practices into the team culture
	• Technical Training – invest in people
	  • Offer technical training for teams to stay current
	  • Identify specific technical trainings to satisfy the architectural runway items
	• Agile Training & Focus on Team Responsibilities
	  • Training for key roles; i.e., Scrum Developer, Product Management, Scrum Master, Architects, etc.

Figure 5-1. Summary of Team Development and Agile Practices Pillar

This pillar should become a major goal to attack in every organization. While it requires investment, without it, progress will be slow. Investment in this area will play a big role in improving morale, building the right product, and delivering value to customers.

Focusing on quality and caring about individuals' development is refreshing to all and a major morale booster. Leadership should be held accountable in delivering continuous improvement in elevating talent in the organization!

Pillar 2: Code Quality and Modernizing Architecture

In many products, teams deal with legacy code where standard code-development practices were not followed. That is usually highlighted as the single biggest challenge when teams are interviewed as to why there is not an effective continuous integration (CI) process. Many examples are shared where code is copied and pasted throughout the code base. This is usually because not all developers have the history and background to confidently remove unused code. Copy-and-pasted pieces of code could be a recipe for missing propagated changes in all sections when updates are made.

Test Coverage

Legacy code is not always documented well. As a result, regular code optimization and cleanup is difficult to conduct. Existing unit test and functional automated tests are also difficult to debug and update. Often, their coverage and effectiveness is questioned, but there is no quick and easy way to find out. Reviewing the list of escaped defects, performing RCCA, and creating a heat map of various modules within the code to ensure good test coverage is an effective approach to take. Ensuring test-strategy discussions take place for every release is another critical item in the test-coverage analysis and improvement approach. I often refer to this comprehensive approach as the *Law of Testing Coverage!*

Good Code Architecture

Good code quality and architecture are key foundational items in software Agile quality. Without investing in a solid architecture and following best code-development practices (i.e., code reviews, unit tests, and integration testing), additional technical debt is guaranteed to be built over time.

Architecture is hard to change and deserves attention. I have heard people say that in Agile, architecture will emerge on its own as teams are self-organized and have freedom to decide how to architect their code. That is not entirely true. Architects play a big role in Agile technology organizations. There is a direct correlation between a good architecture (and good practices) and delivering value to the customers.

While each team has autonomy in designing their code, there needs to be a higher-level focus on the overall product architecture. Think of it as a big map that allows you to manage your vision and get the business value that your customers look for. It focuses on ensuring all modules interconnect and operate together. Keeping up with new technologies and ensuring the architecture adapts to change will pave the road for future success.

Legacy Code

Dealing with legacy code is often difficult, as code cleanup could take a long time. This is why it is important to give priority to developing high-quality new code before addressing the quality of legacy code. If you stop the bleeding by not introducing a new set of technical debt, that by itself is a big step forward toward higher quality.

The single most-critical factor impacting the inability to release software on a frequent cadence is suboptimal code quality. There are usually only a handful of people that have been with the organization for a very long time and know the history and background of the specific piece of legacy code. This by itself can create a significant challenge and leads to not being able to train new engineers quickly and efficiently. It is necessary for teams to ensure they have effective training programs, perform code cleanup, and enhance automated regression test suites with proper priority in their backlog for every release.

Because the impact of suboptimal code is visible via escalations and customer feedback, the leadership team usually understands the importance of making the necessary investment in code cleanup. If they don't, you can always use the same technique that I covered in one of the examples in the previous chapter to do a cost-benefit analysis. That is done by collecting data about the level of effort spent by all functions to deal with escalations and manual efforts to test the code. You can think of that approach as the *Law of Quality Cost Estimation and Benefit!*

Focusing on developing good-quality new code—and in parallel adding backlog items to clean up legacy code over time—is an effective way to prevent new technical debt from forming while having plans to address legacy code.

Creating a quality feature to track this important effort is an excellent way to ensure continuous focus on this very important pillar for the organization.

Example of a Feature to Track Against the Second Pillar of Quality

As a product team member, we need to modernize and simplify our current code architecture, improve code quality, ensure all modules and third-party software versions are current, improve test and code coverage, and ensure new software is built with the best code-development practices in mind.

<u>*Success criteria are:*</u>

- *Enforce coding standards and give testability of the code a high priority for all newly developed code.*

- *Utilize static and dynamic code-analysis tools to gather baseline.*

- *Create backlog items to address high-priority code violations, removal of unused code/duplicate, etc.*

- *Ensure list of major components/modular/TPSRs (third-party software requests) that need updates is reviewed and backlog items are created to address as per priority.*

Figure 5-2 shows a summary of the second Navid's Quality Pillar.

2. Code Quality & architecture	

Code & architectural modularization allow for best test strategy and higher quality	**• Static and Dynamic Code Analysis**
	  • Gather baseline
	  • Code violations, duplicate code, etc.
	  • Level of code modularization
	• New Code
	  • Adhere to code standards with regular code reviews
	  • Define and enforce code architecture (i.e., testability)
	• Legacy Code
	  • Comply with code architecture and code cleanup requirements

Figure 5-2. *Summary of Code Quality and Modernizing Architecture Pillar*

Without good code quality and a solid architecture, progress on continuous process improvement will be limited.

Pillar 3: Focus on Agile Productivity Tools and Quality Enablers

Reliable build and deployment infrastructures are key productivity elements for enhancing internal agility. Being able to receive quick feedback on check-ins with appropriate levels of automation should be part of our DNA. Being predictable with our releases requires us to have a clear Definition of Ready and Definition of Done and ensures consistent execution against set goals.

There is a direct correlation between organizations that have higher internal productivity and use solid software development practices and effective tools, and delivering value to customers. Hence, stronger business and higher revenue. Solid automation and test strategy, faster build time, better debugging tools, and an effective CI process will improve productivity. They are also key elements to building in quality.

DevOps

The word *DevOps* gained momentum a few years back and it is still going strong. If you search online for DevOps, you will get bombarded with information and specific tools offered by various vendors. DevOps removes bottlenecks from Agile teams and can make Agile more Agile! Having a solid DevOps strategy and implementation is similar to having a good railroad infrastructure so your trains are not slowed down and can move fast to deliver value. A great read about IT and DevOps and how they can help your business win is *The Phoenix Project* by Gene Kim, Kevin Behr, and George Spafford.[1]

Optimizing the Build Process

The build process for one of the teams in an organization that I worked for was taking over 36 hours! That meant from the time that a developer checked in a piece of code, it took her 36 hours to find out if her code broke the build. This immediately caught my attention. We needed to find out the root cause of delay for builds that were taking so long to be made available. In addition, since unit testing was not part of the culture of that team, breaking the build after so many hours was not an unusual phenomena! Baselining every quality-impacting factor should be the focus of every quality-passionate individual. I like to refer to this process as another law to remember, the *Law of Baselining Quality Metrics!*

A team of engineers with proper build expertise got together and performed a value-stream analysis to understand what could be done short term versus long term to reduce waste. By focusing on just a few low-hanging items, such as using a set of more powerful build servers, eliminating sequential builds on multiple platforms, allowing a build to continue after capturing a warning message, and a few other improvements, build time reduced by 80 percent! A list of long-term improvement items related to processes and tools were also added to the backlog to continuously improve on.

---

[1]Portland, OR: IT Revolution Press, 2013.

DoR/DoD

Additional productivity-enhancing items, such as updating and attending to DoR and DoD, can have a significantly positive impact on the productivity of the organization. During every release planning, iteration planning, and end-of-iteration demo, DoD and DoR items can get reviewed and healthy discussions can take place if deviations are noticed by the team. Over time, the culture will start to change, and teams won't need as many reminders.

In the world of Agile, there is no longer a separate large QA organization that would perform big chunks of manual test execution at the end of each phase. Automation needs to be an integral part of the process, and scrum teams are encouraged to trim as much manual fat as possible.

Having said all of that, it is important not to get carried away and start introducing too many lightweight tools to replace manual tests. This could create a nightmare for maintenance and root-cause identification. Sometimes when an automated test fails, scrum-team members will have to manually log a defect for the system team to figure out where in the build pipeline the failure resides. Depending on the number of tools and type of tools used, the debugging can almost wipe out the automation savings. Striking the right balance is challenging but doable. This is where using the automation economy approach (see previous chapter) by considering the effect of automated processes and the level of support and maintenance will provide insight into the best path forward. You can remember this approach as the *Law of Automation Economy!*

In order to be successful in the Agile quality journey, we have to agree that certain foundations must be covered in our mindset and processes. Since with limited time and people it is not possible to attend to all technical debt items at once, performing a value-stream analysis is a key step forward. I have found the following three major areas related to this pillar to be popular with most organizations:

- Build process and a meaningful DevOps toolchain
- Test coverage and automation practices and mindset
- DoD/DoR and transparency

Long Tail/Hardening

The preceding key elements (along with a few others) are also responsible for a long tail/hardening for releases with legacy code. Analyzing what and why certain activities are planned for the tail/hardening phase of the release will provide an opportunity to focus on areas to streamline. In one of the examples we covered earlier in the book, PSM was a critical contributing factor to a long tail. Another obvious area is lack of automated tests and the need to perform manual testing. This holistic approach of determining critical factors and optimizing them is simple yet very effective. I like to refer to it as the *Law of Long Tail!*

A great way to keep focus on all productivity-impacting factors for this pillar is to create a feature and track progress against it.

Example of a Feature to Track Against the Third Pillar of Quality

As a product team member, we need to modernize and simplify our build and deployment processes. Optimizing internal processes and adopting solid DoR/DoD and automation strategy will allow for higher productivity and speed.

Success criteria are:

Baseline for DevOps Capability Model is understood and plans for key improvements are prioritized in the backlog (i.e., CI/CD). For example:

- *Build time is reduced.*

- *Effective automation framework for CI/Functional/Performance is in place.*

- *Regression tests are prioritized for automation.*

- *Clear DoD and DoR are established and adhered to for program increment, iteration, and story success (i.e., zero defects for new code and automation, code analysis and downstream impact, burn-down charts, test execution, code coverage, working software, and effective code review process are enforced).*

Figure 5-3 shows the summary of the third Navid's Pillar of Quality.

3. Productivity & Quality Enablers	
Reliable build, solid process, deployment infrastructure, and an effective CI/CD are key to success **Avoid new tech debt**	**• Build/Tool/Deployment** • Continuous integration • Nightly regression • Deployment on servers • Branch strategy (Measuring each step to improve) **• Automation** • Framework for CI, Functional, Performance • Regression tests prioritized for automation • Trending charts available **• Definition of Done (DoD)** • Clear DoD for Story/PI & Sprint success • Interdependencies/interlocks identified • Defect analysis and downstream impact • Burn-down charts for sprint/PI, test exec, defects, code coverage, automation, etc.

Figure 5-3. Summary of Agile Productivity Tools and Quality Enablers Pillar

In order to be successful in the Agile journey, we have to have certain foundations covered in our processes and mindset. Automation, defect reduction, and story/sprint/release success criteria are among the items that many organizations have adopted and made progress with in their continuous process-improvement journey.

Pillar 4: Integrate Various Abilities (Non-Functional Areas) into the Product Development Process

Feedback from internal scrum teams, customer-facing teams, and external customers usually points you to many challenges in various categories of "abilities." For example, when customers are challenged during the upgrade process and do not have proper documentation to walk them through and get unblocked, they would highlight that as poor quality. Performance-related issues that prevent them from scaling their business, vulnerabilities in the code, functional complexity, lack of interoperability and integration with other software, and accessibility limitations show up as poor quality when customers are interviewed and asked for their feedback.

These are usually the last areas that most product teams focus on, unless they are integrated into their development process. Training for some of those areas, such as internationalizing the code or making the code accessible, should be part of the education and development plan for engineering team members.

When talking with the Support department, customers sometimes complain about the fact that self-diagnostic approaches are not considered in the design, error messages are not self-explanatory, and call home and telemetry features are not prioritized. Those all come under the umbrella of Supportability and need to be addressed.

Usability is another important element in today's world. Purchasing software used to be done based on a checklist. A list of features and capabilities were highlighted as line items, and the buyer would check them off based on certain documentation, but users were not a part of that decision-making process. Today, the buyer is most likely the user. Usability for working software is one of the key criteria for customers today.

Each product team may highlight a different pain point as their major "abilities" category of challenge. It is essential for each team to do a detailed analysis of each area, create a baseline, prioritize the highest-impacting ones in their backlog, and regularly provide progress in each area. Ultimately, teams want to get to a point where every "ability" is built into the process and overhead is minimized. But creating a clear roadmap to address the highest-impacting ones first will be the best approach.

The ownership for this pillar usually relies with the architects. Once architects internalize the importance of this pillar, they need to ensure sufficient architectural spikes are created and prioritized in the backlog for teams to focus on.

The following quality feature can be used as an example to help product teams keep focus on this important quality-impacting pillar.

Example of a Feature to Track Against the Fourth Pillar of Quality

As a product development team, it is important to integrate the abilities into our product cadence to address key internal and external customer needs and help reduce TCO (Total Cost of Ownership).

Success criteria are:

- *Backlog item is created to review all categories of abilities.*

- *Customer feedback and other TCO (total cost of ownership) analysis reviewed and highest-priority items are highlighted to be addressed by teams.*

- *Baseline document created and gaps identified.*

- *Specific stories are created to be worked on throughout the release.*

Figure 5-4 Summarizes the fourth Navid's Quality Pillar.

4. Integrate Abilities	

Major categories to focus on with clear team ownership for all:
• Supportability
• Scalability
• Securability
• Upgradability/Installability
• Localizability
• Usability
• Accessibility
• Integratability
• Interoperability
• Platform Supportability
	• **Baseline**
	  • Complete assessment in each area
	  • Focus on the highest-impacting ones and add to backlog
	
	• **Continuous Process Improvement (CPI)**
	  • Trending scorecard to be filled out every PI

Figure 5-4. Summary of Integrating the Non-Functional/Abilities in Software Development Process Pillar

Key abilities impacting NPS and TCO that are commonly prioritized in the backlog by most teams are listed below, but depending on the maturity of the product teams, they do vary over time:

- Integrability
- Upgradability
- Securability

Pillar 5: Ensure Customer Success—Voice of the Customer in Everything We Do Every Day!

Customer engagement and putting them at the center of everything we do are key to every organization's success. The voice of the customer plays a big role in ensuring that we build a relevant solution for our customers. Delivering quality releases on a predictable cadence to solve customer issues is our ultimate goal.

Earlier, I shared an example of an organization where, after teams had spent many months of hard work on a new set of features to release to the market, they were told at the final stages of the release that the release was canceled. This was a great example where the need for creating a new feature was not validated with customers. There is nothing more demoralizing to a team than knowing that they had been working so hard on features that were not even relevant to customers.

Even more disappointing is when teams release a version of the software and the adoption rate is very low due to perceived quality issues, such as a difficult upgrade process or regression in basic functionality.

The Dev/Buddy program that got established in one of the organizations I worked in resonated extremely well with external customers and generated lots of positive energy with the internal teams. Learning directly from customers what their needs were, what they viewed as a great outcome, and how they were willing to partner with the product teams to create a good solution was extremely refreshing. I like to refer to this as the *Law of Voice of the Customer and Tour de Product!*

In many organizations, the culture of leveraging the views of internal customers does not exist. We often forget that departments such as Support, Professional Services, Pre-sales, and SWAT work with customers regularly and have great insight into what will help in creating a strong solution for them. Building a culture of engaging internal customer-facing departments should be given a high priority. In fact, reviewing NPS scores should be considered the responsibility of all functions in an organization and not just a selected team or function. Looking at the provided feedback from different lenses will provide additional insight that can be incorporated in the existing or future versions of the product.

Support/Engineering interlock can provide great visibility into challenges that exist on both sides. Often there are frustrations reported in those departments due to lack of visibility and understanding of how customer issues are handled. I have seen rotational programs for both functions make a huge difference in strengthening the relationship among those teams and enhancing collaboration to help attend to the common goal of resolving customer issues effectively. I often refer to these types of engagements as the *Law of Collaboration with Customer-Facing Organizations*.

Another area of concern is the lack of focus on a holistic TCO. Often, only the internal costs are considered, and the customer's TCO is ignored. Initiatives that reduce TCO internally may unknowingly raise TCO on the customer side. This creates tension and is often perceived as low quality. This is where focusing on the Worldview and Quality Integral Map process will help in identifying a collective list of TCO. The list can then get prioritized and incorporated in the backlog for internal teams to work on.

The following feature template can help teams create customer-related stories to be worked on in various iterations. This will ensure focus on this important quality pillar by having relevant stories available to be picked up in various iterations and be continuously improved upon.

Example of a Feature to Track Against the Fifth Pillar of Quality

As a product team, we want to ensure customer success by bringing the voice of the customer into every decision we make every day!

Success criteria are:

- *Backlog item is created to establish a baseline for the NPS highest-impacting factors:*
  - *Number of fixes required per customer per year, MTTR, customer defect backlog, customer hot spots, etc.*
  - *Prioritize agreed-upon NPS highest contributors in the backlog to address.*
  - *Create a baseline for the TCO highest-impacting factors (i.e., deployment, upgrade complexity, etc.).*
  - *Prioritize items in the backlog to address.*

- *Customer validation:*
  - *Active customer participation in sprint reviews*
  - *Feature/charter approval*
  - *Tour de "product" with customers to learn their specific use cases*
  - *Use customer data (with their consent) to do internal upgrade testing to understand potential challenges.*

Figure 5-5 summarizes the fifth Navid's Quality Pillar.

5. Ensure Customer Success	
Bring the voice of the customer into our product development processes	**NPS-impacting Factors:** • Number of fixes required per customer per year • MTTR • Regularly review and address customer hot spots **Customer Validation:** • Active customer participation in sprint reviews • New features, user experience, and major visible bug fixes • Exploratory testing by customer-interfacing teams **Customer Health:** • Upgrades, new installs, Number of older releases **TCO** • Pick top contributor and address per program increment (i.e., deployment)

Figure 5-5. *Summary of Engraving the Voice of Customers in Everything We Do Everyday Pillar*

Focusing on this pillar is the responsibility of the entire organization, but is tracked and measured by the Support department in various categories. Having awareness and plans to address each category will be the responsibility of the proper respective function (i.e., PM, Engineering, and Support).

In summary, it is important to be mindful of the fact that we build software to solve customer problems. Measuring the value they gain by using our solution and capturing their experience along the way will ensure success. The Agile quality framework that I have defined in this chapter can be used in every organization to help with their holistic Agile quality transformation.

Various angles of quality have been considered in the five Quality Pillars, which I summarize here.

Navid's Quality Pillars (NQPs):

1. Team Development and Agile Practices
2. Code Quality and Architecture
3. Agile Productivity and Quality Enablers
4. Abilities
5. Customer Success

I have also referred to a few laws to remember as approaches that can aid teams in determining how and where to invest and continuously improve on their Agile quality. These approaches can be extended to other organizations with similar challenges.

Navid's Ten Laws of Agile Quality:

1. Law of Quality Cost Estimation and Benefits
2. Law of Baselining Quality Metrics
3. Law of Automation Economics
4. Law of Engaging Global Teams
5. Law of Effective Testing Coverage
6. Law of Horrific Reference Stack (PSM)
7. Law of Conservation of Long Tail or Hardening phase
8. Law of Voice of the Customer and Tour de "Product"
9. Law of Continuous Learning (and Unlearning)
10. Law of Collaboration with Customer-Facing Organizations

Self-Reflection Questions

- What are the five NQPs (Navid's Quality Pillars)?

- Why is it important to define such pillars?

- What are abilities?

- Can you name a few items that are covered as total cost of ownership (TCO) internally and on the customer side?

- Why will having a solid DevOps process help quality?

- Discuss the importance of having customers at the center.

- Why is suboptimum code quality a reason for a long hardening phase and escalation challenges?

- What is the role of automation in the predictability of releases?

- Why is investing in people and elevating their skills related to product quality?

- What are the Laws of Agile Quality defined by Navid?

Assessment Against NQPs (Navid's Quality Pillars)

Vision, Strategy, Execution, Measurement (VSEM)

Now that we have defined the five Navid's Quality Pillars (NQPs), we need to focus on how to best operationalize them across multiple product teams in both a business unit and an enterprise. Creating a visual radiator to help and remind everyone of the overall quality vision, strategy, execution, and measurements (VSEM) is usually an effective next logical step. The one-page summary in Figure 6-1 can be posted in multiple sites and near high-traffic areas to ensure it generates discussions and ideas start to flow. In one particular organization, we needed the transformation teams to help the rest of the organization adopt and implement these strategies. This visual radiator was a great reminder and reference sheet to which the entire business unit could refer.

© CA 2019
N. Nader-Rezvani, *An Executive's Guide to Software Quality in an Agile Organization*,
https://doi.org/10.1007/978-1-4842-3751-9_6

Business Unit Quality Improvement Plan (VSEM)

Vision
- Deliver high-quality releases on a regular cadence to solve customer problems and be a leader in the industry
- Enforce modern product development best practices moving forward and identify critical areas to continuously improve on
- Focus on items that will align with our Agile transformation goals

	1) People and skillsets	2) Code modernization and code quality	3) Drive Agile productivity tools and processes	4) Integrate abilities into our product cadence	5) Ensure customer success
Strategic Pillars	• Ensure proper skillsets & Agile roles exist to deliver against roadmap and product quality • Invest in people and training • Ensure software development hygiene is internalized by all	• Adhere to code standards and architecture for new code • Comply with code cleanup requirements	• Standardize build/deployment processes • Adhere to the DoD & DoR and ensure automation is engraved into our DNA	• Continuous process improvement in prioritized categories of abilities to ensure customer success and satisfaction	• Voice of the customers to be integrated into our development processes • Special focus on TCO/NPS impacting factors • Utilize telemetry
Execution	• Ensure skills are matched with backlog for products • Fill gaps and provide training to elevate teams • Define roles and responsibilities as per Agile recommendations	• Focus on modularization of code base and exposure of RESTful APIs • Implement code quality assessment tools and identify priorities to work on	• Create a baseline for build and other development processes (i.e., automation, nightly regression, etc.) and areas to improve • Clear definition and agreement on DoD & DoR	• Publish abilities scorecard & Identify the top items impacting TCO/NPS that will be a focus for the next 3 PIs (i.e., Upgradability, Scalability, Securability, etc.)	• Identify items from the volume-driver analysis that are prioritized in the backlog • Include internal/external customers in PI charter review, EoS demos and hands-on testing • Know customer install base
Measure (What does success look like?)	• A pro forma is created and agreed upon by the triad • Specific training, certification, and hiring plans are in place as per the Agile recommendation and product roadmap	• Targeted development/testing approach with higher confidence over time • Continuous improvement on code quality metrics	• Continuous Integration and nightly automated regression builds run and triaged • Build time is baselined and improvement planned • DoD/DoR is followed and improved against	• Specific items reflecting top TCO/NPS factors are prioritized in the backlog with specific plans for the next 3 PIs • Support data over the period of four quarters show improvement	• Hot spots/VDA items are reflected with proper priority in the backlog • Plans for internal exploratory testing are available • Release charter is reviewed with customers • Customers present at EoS demos

Figure 6-1. *Example of a quality VSEM*

Over-communicating the VSEM was the path we took in one business unit. I traveled to multiple development sites, held town halls, answered questions, and met with the transformation team to focus on Agile and quality implementation. Getting the product teams in other geographical locations aligned with our vision and execution plans for the upcoming releases was critical to get everyone on board.

I worked with every product team to ensure buy-in and full understanding of the plan. We discussed at length what each pillar meant to their specific product line as per their maturity level. I also asked them to get together with their triads (product chief architect, engineering lead, product manager) and walk through each pillar to create a baseline in each of the key areas.

For this transformation to be successful, teams needed to buy in on the existing challenges and what goodness looked like for them. I knew well that if we were to be tops-down without getting the product teams and especially the architects and senior leaders/engineers on board, the initiative would not last very long. It was important for teams to do their own assessments and not be told what they needed to do.

Each product team was tasked with the following actions:

- Define what success looks like in each pillar.
- Evaluate where their team is currently with respect to various defined success areas; create a baseline.
- Set quantifiable goals for key areas.
- Track and measure against the set goals.
- Report on their continuous improvement initiatives.
- Rinse and repeat.

It was important to communicate regularly, to reiterate that our Agile and quality excellence journey had begun, and to provide regular updates to the entire organization on a regular cadence. I was given a specific timeslot in every Quarterly All-Hands and Business Review meeting to share updates from teams' progress in their quality transformation journey.

Here were few examples of updates that I provided in the early stages of our transformation:

- **Agile Transformation Initial Focus:**
  - Organizational alignment (people/roles/skills)
  - Agile ceremonies assessment and processes and review survey results
  - Putting customers at the center and incorporate their feedback

- **Agile Transformation Future Focus:**
    - Continue focus on processes to promote quality, organizational alignment, and customer focus
    - Entire value stream around BU-level strategy and focus on driving business agility and prioritization based on metrics such as revenue and strategic value to customers
- **Five NQPs (Navid's Quality Pillars) have been identified:**
    - People/skills, code arch/quality, tools/productivity, abilities, customer engagement
    - Self-assessment has been done by all product teams to be used as baseline
    - Specific items identified to continuously improve on as per product maturity
- **High-priority focused areas for products X, Y, Z:**
    - Automation and test coverage
    - Build-time reduction and automation of steps
    - Streamlining the Product Support Matrix (PSM)
    - Identify integration challenges and attend to them
    - Regular security scans and addressing vulnerabilities along the way
    - Launch upgrade pilot program with customers

Once the journey began and communication at all levels started focusing on holistic quality and Agile adoption across the board, the mindset started to shift. Some people internalized the value in the first few meetings. Others took a bit longer to change their behavior and truly believe in the need to change. Regular communication with the business leaders and the organization as a whole really helped emphasize the fact that commitment existed at all levels. It became obvious that this was not a new wave that would die down if we just ignored it and didn't do anything about it. No one wanted to be highlighted in a large organizational meeting as the team that, despite their known quality issues, was not investing in any of the areas to continuously improve and delight customers.

The scorecard for every team was presented in the Quarterly All-Hands meetings. This ensured visibility into the strategic objectives and follow-up by each product team. It also underlined the leadership team's commitment to focusing on various aspects of quality. At first it was uncomfortable for teams to open up their dirty laundry and share their quality challenges with everyone. A clear message was shared that the objective of openly reviewing teams' quality statuses was to ensure continuous Agile quality improvement was given a high priority. That message was effective, and teams were energized to learn that they were not going to get micro-managed. They performed a fair assessment of their statuses and held themselves accountable for improvement. Knowing where they were in their transformation journey and having solid plans to address issues and focus on outcomes was a game changer for each of the product teams. That helped the organization move down the path of their total quality journey with clear understanding of expectations.

The focus was initially on

- understanding their existing baseline;
- learning what they were considering as their priorities with respect to the quality release metrics;
- ensuring they were reviewing their progress against their set goals; and
- promoting transparency, teamwork, collaboration, and a culture of quality.

As teams got more and more acclimated to the overall quality objectives and started to internalize their impact on both the internal organization and customers, new ideas started to brew. The architecture team started to pay attention to key quality-impacting factors with which they could pave the road within the architectural runway backlog. Items such as integrating open source tools to gain visibility into the code quality started to get more attention from the senior engineering team members. Ideas for standardizing tools across the business unit and focusing on standard APIs to ease integration, operationalizing exploratory role-based testing (XRBT) with the customer-impacting departments, and helping with such initiatives started to draw in a few volunteers. This was a great sense of accomplishment for the entire team.

Getting the architects and senior engineers on board with the initiative was key. They were the ones mentoring the rest of the product teams; they understood the challenges and were able to come up with solutions to address them. They also started to lead by example, holding themselves to high software development standards and holding each other and the rest of the team accountable to ensure attending to quality improvement be part of the culture.

We also provided a few templates and metrics for teams to use. Figure 6-2 is a template that can be used to create a team's baseline and to perform self-assessment against the five NQPs. Figure 6-3 includes example charts that were used by teams to capture their quality-release metrics. Figure 6-4 was used to assess the team's predictability and productivity. Finally, Figure 6-5 captures a simple way to track investment in innovation.

Product X
Improvement on Quality Pillars

■ Q3 ■ Q4

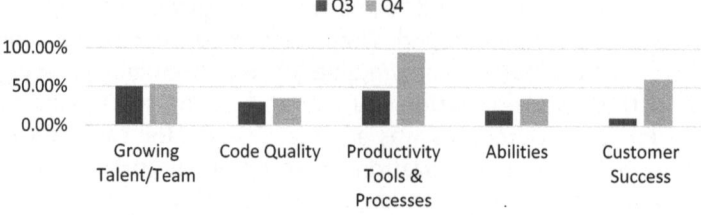

Major Quality Impacting Accomplishments this quarter	Impacting Pillar	% Progress Against Set Goal
Hired SME in xyz	Talent/Team	
Reduced code blockers by 20%	Code Quality	
Automated 200 smoke tests	Productivity	
Attended to top 2 Upgrade Impacting factors	Abilities	
Held RBXT session and identified xblocking issues	Customer Success	

Figure 6-2. Example of a Product Team's Quarterly Assessment against NQPs

Release-Quality Metrics Examples

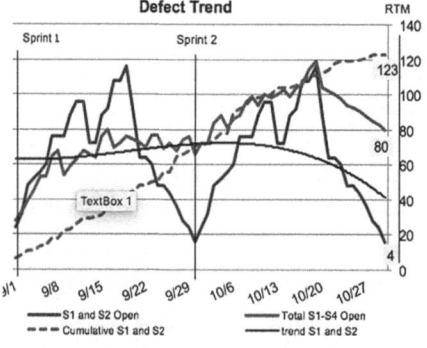

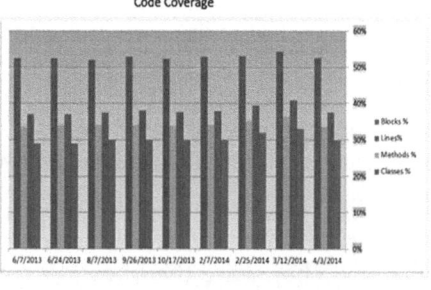

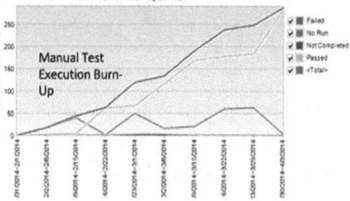

Figure 6-3. Example of release-quality metrics

Team Metrics per Release	Release 1	Release 2	Release 3	Release 4
Release velocity (actual/planned)				
Predictability measure				
Number of features planned/done				
Number of tech debt and arch features				
Number of stories planned/done				
Number of skills/roles filled/gaps				

Figure 6-4. Example of KPIs to help with team's predictability metrics

Release	Q1	Q2	Q3	Q4
X				
Patentable items				
Process innovation				

Figure 6-5. Example of team's innovation metrics

We kept on emphasizing with the entire organization—and especially with a few impatient leaders—the following key concepts:

- This was going to be a long journey.

- Focus was less on ensuring every detailed Agile process was followed and more on the value and outcome for customers.

- It was not possible to address every item from every pillar in one release. But having the assessment and committing to continuous improvement would ensure ongoing focus on quality.

- Transparency, teamwork, and collaboration were non-negotiable.

Self-Reflection Questions

- What is the importance of having a clear VSEM defined for an organization?

- Why is it important for teams to do their own independent quality assessment and come up with an improvement plan?

- If there are many angles of quality that need attention, how would you suggest teams prioritize what to go after first?

- What are some metrics that focus on a team's maturity? Why are they important metrics?

- What are some metrics that you use in your product team for every sprint and release?

- Why are over-communication and transparency important when you try to change the culture?

Agile Quality Test Strategy

Shift Left

This chapter will focus on the overall quality test strategy and its importance in an Agile world. Most Agile product development teams develop on cadence and release on demand. An Agile release may consist of multiple program increments (PIs). Being able to fully test new features and ensure there is no regression in existing ones is always challenging. A clear test strategy should be an integral part of every new feature. Ensuring a quality architect (or a very senior quality-passionate technical individual) is included in conversations when a new feature is discussed will be necessary to get the proper level of attention on this very important topic.

Quality engineers are able to lead the team in understanding how much and what level of testing should be planned for a given feature and a release. These types of discussions at the scrum-team and release-team levels will guide the team in creating appropriate quality-impacting stories and allow for more accurate estimation to be done for every story and feature.

© CA 2019

N. Nader-Rezvani, *An Executive's Guide to Software Quality in an Agile Organization*,
https://doi.org/10.1007/978-1-4842-3751-9_7

Role of a QA Engineer

Before we get into the details of test strategy, it is important to highlight that often quality from a QA perspective suffers more than quality from a developer's perspective. That could be the result of a poor ratio in team compositions, old organizational structures, balancing a new team structure, imbalanced pay, or lack of QA leadership during initial stages.

In the world of Agile, you may have seen controversies about the role of a QA engineer. I have seen examples where QA is used synonymously with a tester. Some believe that since every developer should test his/her own code, there is no need for a QA on a scrum team. Some bad decisions have actually been made where companies got rid of all QA engineers when embarking on the Agile journey, only to find out soon after that they had created a huge skill gap!

I am a firm believer that QA does a lot more than just test and report defects. They play a customer-advocate role and take pride in breaking the code! In most organizations I have been in, there are certain individuals who, even with a strong coding background, prefer to break the code before our customers do so! They are proud of their QA profession and work very well with the developers on their scrum team to promote the test-first approach. They should be considered as an equal member of a scrum team and not be viewed as second-class citizens.

It is important for the internal organizational structure to function seamlessly so that we can continue to focus on our customers. A well-designed structure in any organization allows for stronger accountability, breaking down barriers, and more efficient workflow. With that, we can expect superior and high-quality products that deliver value to our customers and lead to better sales and increased revenue.

Having developers and testers working side by side to discuss test strategy and promote test-driven development is critical. There are still far too many organizations with QA teams that are not integrated well with the development teams. As a result, they lag behind the curve and often end up testing a piece of code way after it has been developed. They find issues late in the cycle that could potentially delay the scheduled release date.

I often tell my development teams that QA is your safety net, but they are not expected to find every defect that you put in! Obviously, I don't make best friends when I make such comments, but it is true. It is important for QA to participate in the full testing strategy and to help push the discovery of issues to earlier cycles of code development. That way, QA can focus on corner cases so as to find more-critical bugs and try to really break the code. Often, QA teams are consumed with finding basic defects, which leaves them no time to focus on designing more-complex tests to catch issues internally before customers find them.

I once had to hold a special session with the entire Development/QA department to share the breakdown of issues that were reported from QA testing. I explained that finding issues such as "UI not loading up" is not what I expect QA to spend their valuable time on. Frankly, we needed to create a culture where developers were proud of the quality of the code that they were putting out. I shared an example from my prior job, where one of the senior developers was so proud of his code that if QA found a Severity 1 or 2 issue in his code, he would take them out to lunch! That is the quality mindset we need—not one where developers hurriedly develop a piece of code and throw it over the fence to QA to find basic issues.

Promoting Healthy Competition

The notion of producing high-quality code that a developer is proud of got a lot of attention in one organization that I was a part of. A healthy competition started to gain momentum. Developers decided to hold each other accountable, and with every build-failure notification, the responsible person would get bombarded with messages through the internal social media tool. While part of it was having some fun at the workplace, it actually influenced good practices. The test-first approach became more popular, code reviews were taken more seriously, and test-strategy discussions took place more frequently.

Shift Left

The concept of "shifting left" is not new, but it has not yet been fully adopted in many organizations. The whole idea of finding issues earlier in the cycle to reduce costs and remove quality risks needs to be internalized. When issues are found late in the cycle, fixing such issues could actually de-stabilize the code and introduce new defects. It could put teams in a spiral cycle and delay their software delivery. Figure 7-1 shows how the cost of finding and resolving issues later in the development cycle is exponentially higher than finding and fixing them earlier. Shifting left and finding defects earlier not only helps with cost optimization—it also reduces cycle time and ultimately creates a better customer experience.

Shifting Defect Detection Left in Development Lifecycle

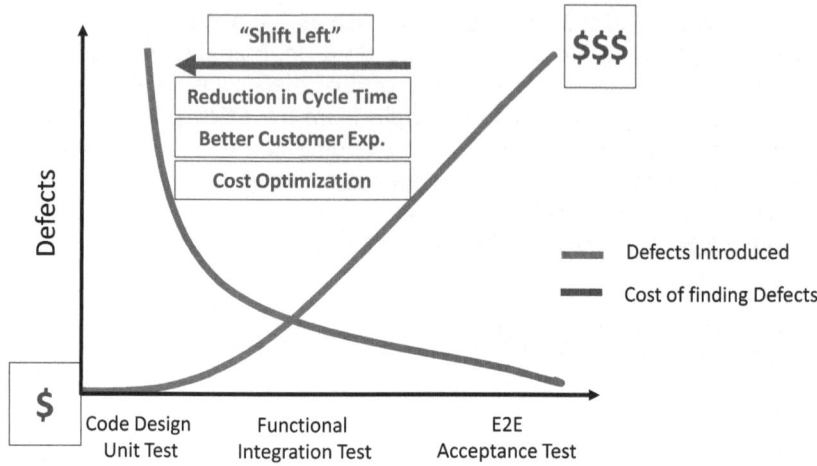

Figure 7-1. "Shift Left" cost benefit

Having a solid test strategy along with having good software development practices are considered basic steps in improving the customer experience. Software test automation is no longer a luxury and is considered a necessity to deliver value faster with built-in quality. Removing the responsibility of finding defects from our customers' plates will certainly improve customer satisfaction and the Net Promoter Survey score, which leads to a healthier business!

There are two phases where test-strategy discussions are critical:

- Ongoing feature backlog grooming
- Program increment (release) planning

To create a culture where the entire team contributed to the overall test strategy, one organization I was in created a test-strategy template for every feature. The idea was to initiate test-related discussions early on when a new feature was being groomed. For example, if a new test-automation tool was needed, a test-automation spike story would get created before the framework was implemented.

The following default story template can be used for every relevant feature.

Template for a Default Test-Strategy Story

As a quality stakeholder, I recognize the need for a solid test strategy that is documented and followed by all teams.

This story may result in additional spike stories. The purpose of this strategy is to ensure testing and automation approaches gain the required level of visibility and investment. It addresses following key aspects:

1. Scope (i.e., what type of testing is required and what can be excluded?)

2. Tools and techniques (automation and manual)

3. Environments (including test data)

4. Dependencies, risks, and mitigation

5. Execution strategy and milestones

Acceptance Criteria:

I know this is done when:

1. Testing strategy for feature is created.

2. Scope is validated (i.e., including regression testing).

3. Release team and triads have approved it.

Testing Strategy

People often say that in Agile there is no need to create a test plan. I agree that creating a very elaborate test plan with exacting details is not needed in Agile development. However, having a clear understanding of what tests are needed, communicating the scope with the release team, and saving it in a shared location are important. I always use the example of going on a trip. If you don't have a master plan, including what airline you are taking, where you will be staying, and what activities you would like to do, you may have difficulty even getting to your destination. The "master plan" is the test strategy; the "destination" is a quality release.

This section will cover various types of testing, why they are important, and how they should be considered in your master test strategy. It will provide a solid framework from which teams can derive their test strategy. The objectives of the Agile quality test strategy are to do the following:

- Provide a framework for testing within the development lifecycle so that the effort stays focused and on schedule.

- Identify the tasks necessary to prepare for and to conduct release-level manual and automated tests across teams.

- Forgo a traditional siloed approach of testing, and instead communicate clearly and frequently and coordinate with all members on the Agile Release Team.

- Items to communicate include which teams have added specific stories to their product backlog, and subsequently to their iteration backlog. This includes coordination of testing activities to avoid duplication of effort and reduce the opportunity for errors to occur.

- Ensure sharing of test data throughout the layers of testing.

- Represent functional and non-functional requirements of the product/component and ensure those requirements have been met.

- If the project has a third-party or open-source component, then the stories derived should indicate clearly who is performing functional, stress, and system testing and should specify the acceptance criteria for the component.

When developing a test strategy, be sure to consider the following:

- Milestone expectations. For example, there may be specific requirements to achieve major milestones, such as customer demo, platform certification, infrastructure requirements, etc., that need to be considered.

- Ensure the program increment/release objectives are clearly understood and are taken into consideration when creating a holistic test strategy.

- Use a test-driven development (TDD) approach with strong emphasis on automation from the early stages of the release.

- Determine test methodology/ies that will be most effective in finding critical defects early and efficiently. Perform API testing or command-line testing to test code earlier in the cycle instead of relying only on "black box" testing. Consider how best to leverage and integrate static code-analysis tools for early detections.

- Approaches may include risk-based testing, change-based testing, requirements-based testing, scenario-based testing, story-based testing, model-based testing, attack-based testing, fault injection, exploratory testing, and so on.

- Expertise and the tools available to the team for testing

- How you will approach regression testing. A brand-new product might be different than an existing product with a large number of automated tests available. Certain functionality in released products may be field proven, and if nothing was changed, the risk of regressions may be minimal.

- Strongly consider change-based testing with a clear heat map to indicate where the additional focus is needed. Keep in mind that there may not be enough time to run through the entire regression test suite.

- Dependencies, risks, and gaps—ROAMing (Resolve, Own, Accept, or Mitigate) exercise will identify risks and actions necessary to include in the test strategy. For example, if a major component will be deprecated, it is important to clearly state what level of regression testing will be needed to assess potential collateral damage.

Several testing types are provided as examples in the following sections. Utilize these test-strategy guidelines where applicable and add any other test types that are appropriate to your strategy.

It is also critical to fully understand the different types of testing and their various layers so as to apply the best test strategy for the different stages of feature development. The foundation starts at the unit-test level at the bottom, and as code becomes more stable, additional layers are expected to be designed and executed.

A combination of continuous automated tests, blending in testing techniques, integrating code coverage, and utilizing analytics to focus on impacted regression will give you a solid testing strategy. Without a proper test-automation strategy, a continuous-testing model will not be effective or even possible. It is also important to consider the integration of static code analysis in the testing model so early detection is made possible.

Testing Layers

It is important for teams to acknowledge that it is physically impossible for test professionals to validate every configuration and scenario. Strategizing the appropriate level of testing at each stage of development is key to ensuring proper coverage is achieved. The risk of not covering certain test combinations will have to be discussed and internalized by the product teams.

We all have seen several variations of the Test Pyramid that was introduced by Martin Fowler and Michael Cohn.[1] One example is reflected in Figure 7-2. The major takeaway is that teams should focus on producing many more low-level unit tests than high-level UI-based automated and manual tests, including exploratory and usability testing. This test-layer framework is used for continuous integration and continuous delivery, which are critical to unlocking the benefits of Agile testing.

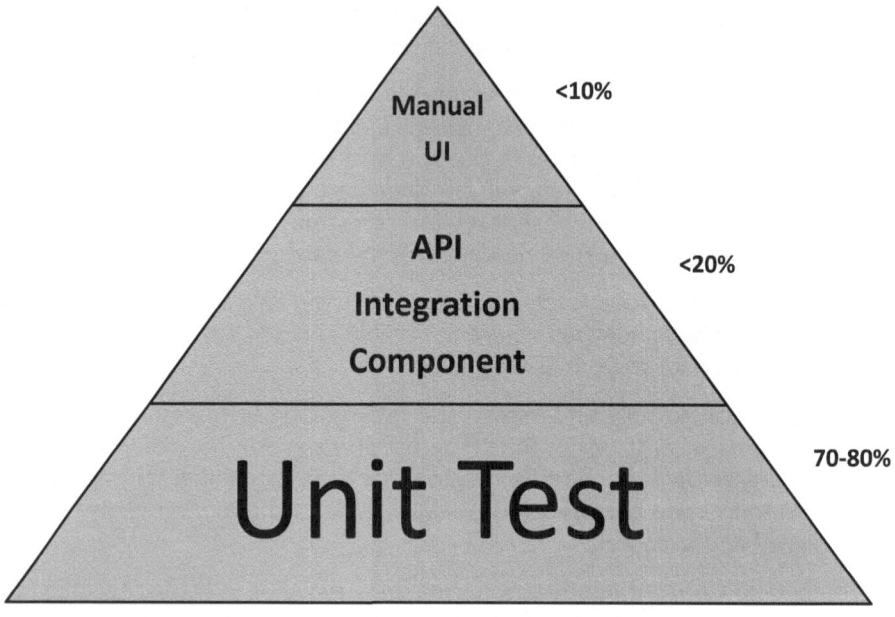

Figure 7-2. Test Pyramid

In reality, though, many organizations have an automated test framework similar to that shown in Figure 7-3, where a majority of the focus is on the manual and UI automated tests. This is referred to as the Ice Cream Cone of Testing! This does not allow for a successful CI/CD model, which is a prerequisite to having a continuous test model with good coverage. Such teams don't invest time in developing unit tests, because it is not "easy" to do so. What they don't realize is that solid implementation of automated unit-test coverage will save lots of money and time by finding issues earlier in the development cycle.

---

[1]https://martinfowler.com/articles/practical-test-pyramid.html

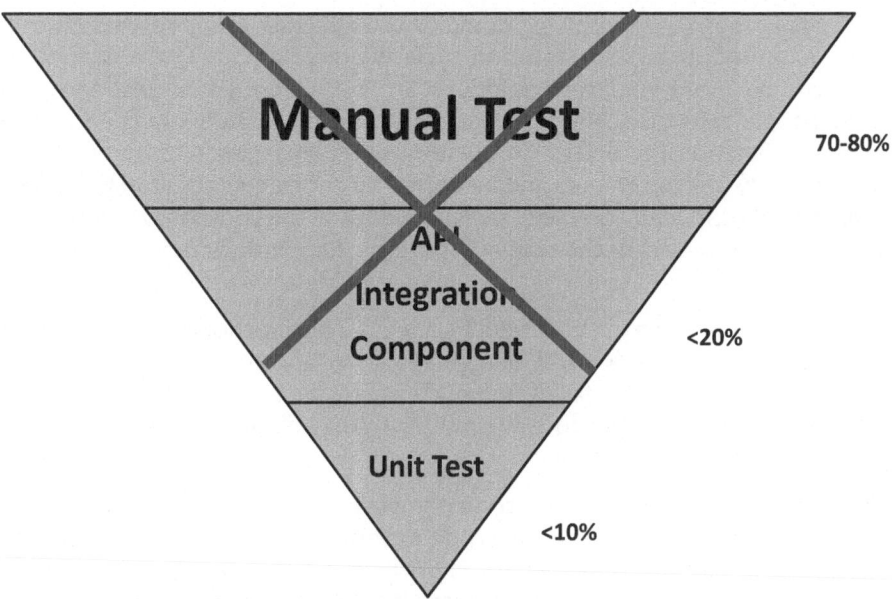

Figure 7-3. Ice Cream Cone of Testing

Impacted Regression Testing

Once, I heard from a sales team member who was confused as to why we were spending so much time discussing the test strategy for new features. He said: "It is simple in my mind—for every new feature, build a complete test suite that exercises the entire codebase and then execute them continuously!" I was speechless; if we could do that so simply, we could send all of our experienced test engineers home! I carefully explained to him that 100 percent coverage is extremely time consuming and expensive and that we would never have time to run all the tests for the release. It is important to consider all types of testing to get the best coverage possible, and discussing details around that will ensure high test coverage and better quality.

With applications' ever-growing complexity, expecting every regression test to be executed in a short iteration cycle is not practical. There is a lot of emphasis on more-intelligent solutions around change-based testing or, as some people refer to it, impacted regression testing. Change in the form of increased functionality brings on additional risk that needs to get carefully analyzed. New enhancements and increased functionalities result in additional interdependencies and complexities. Knowledge of the codebase and properly training new members of the team will be key in fully understanding the impact of new changes.

I am sure you have heard comments such as: "This functionality is no longer working today. I made a small change yesterday and tested it locally, but it wasn't related to what is failing today." Testing is not a trivial task and is the main reason why we need to elevate test-strategy discussions during feature grooming and release planning.

Understanding the architecture, code complexity, amount of legacy code, and what each test covers; measuring code coverage; and focusing on designing tests that validate new changes are important. That knowledge can then be used to create a strategy that is internalized by all scrum teams and triads to ensure proper time and investment is allocated and all testing angles are considered.

Test Levels

Figure 7-4 provides a high-level summary of various testing levels.

Layered Test Coverage

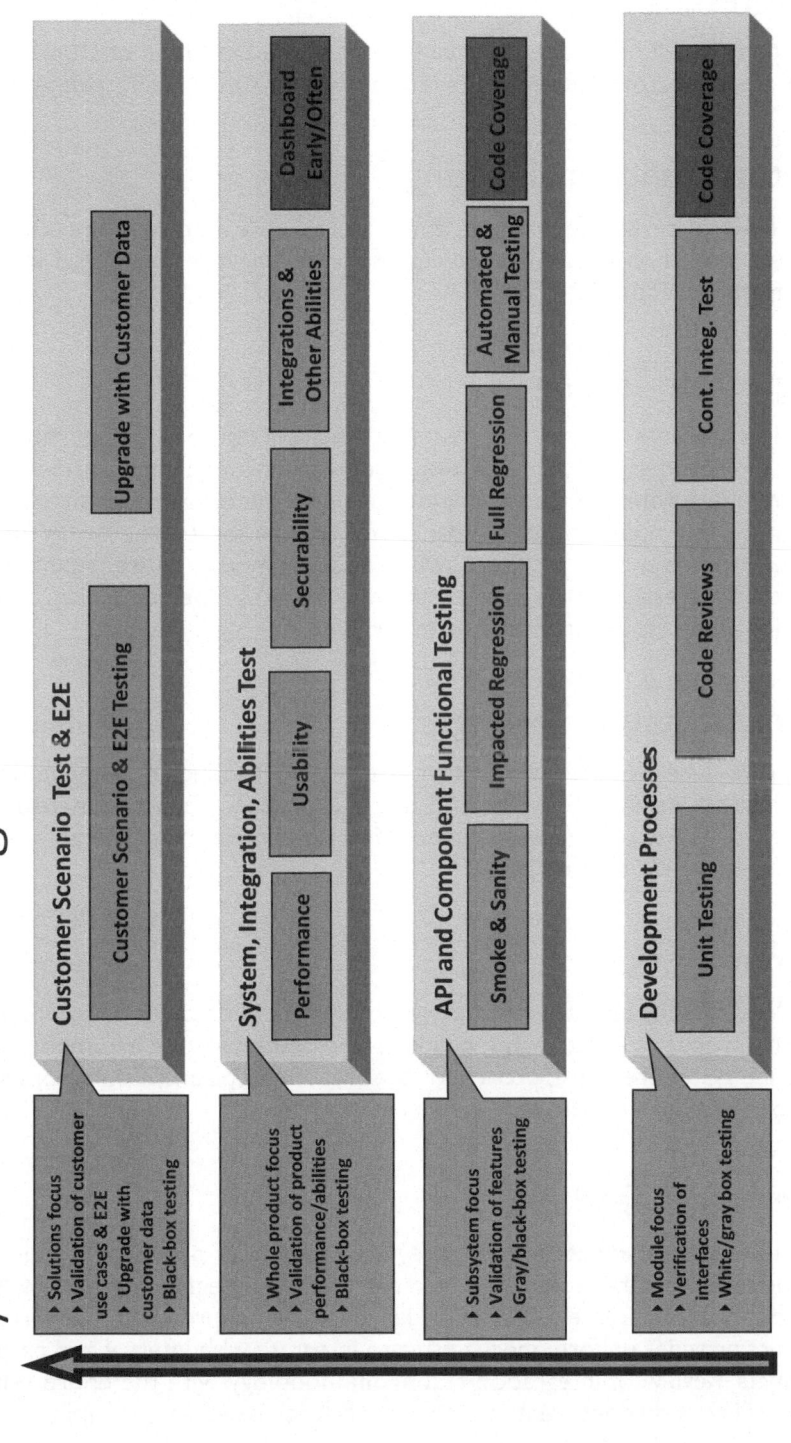

Figure 7-4. Layered test coverage

Unit Testing

Unit tests for all new code need to be part of the Definition of Done, and as such, are mandatory. Code-coverage tools will validate the effectiveness.

Feature/Functional Testing

This layer of testing focuses on the features at a module, component, or product level. It ensures impacted regression testing is incorporated with the new feature testing.

Regression Testing

This level focuses on ensuring new functionality/feature does not introduce bugs or negatively impact existing product functionality. Consider using continuous automated testing focused around the areas of change as new features are implemented. Guidance for regression-testing areas usually comes from the QA architect, with input from the entire scrum team. Impacted-regression strategy to ensure new features have not broken existing functionalities should be discussed in detail.

Documentation Testing

Testing will be done to verify that user-visible product documentation is sufficient to install, administer, and use the product. Each scrum team has the responsibility to review documentation for completeness and accuracy as new functionality is developed.

System Testing

This level focuses on testing the integrated system of modules or components within a product area to verify it produces the desired results. It is important to describe system-testing approach for the areas in scope and ensure consistent approach across the release.

Integration Testing

This level focuses on testing the integrated system of products or solutions (including third-party software) to verify that the integrated products meet the desired requirements. It provides a testing approach to ensure the product provides uniform mechanisms to integrate with internal and external products. Review of integration-testing methodology with the entire release team will provide consistent testing approach across various scrum teams.

E2E Customer Scenario Testing

Also referred to as Business Process Testing or Model-Based Testing, it should include external and internal customers.

External:

Establish a customer-validation program to engage at least three customers throughout the release cycle when new features are made available to seek feedback early and often. This will allow customers to run through their E2E use cases and highlight challenges or provide option to enhance the features. Some teams have built partnerships with specific customers and have access to their environment details and dataset to run generic use cases against. This is a great way to test out new features, ensure there are no regressions, and receive early feedback.

Internal:

Exploratory testing by internal customers (i.e., Support, Presales, Professional Services, and SWAT) is a great approach to follow here.

■ **Note**   Consider all test data needed for functional testing and its setup or location in early test-strategy discussions.

Non-Functional (Abilities) Testing

Testing that determines the extent to which the application meets the expected non-functional requirements is often referred to as "abilities."

The following are the specific types of "abilities" that teams should review and consider as per the requirements for their application.

Accessibility Testing

Testing that will be done to ensure that the product/component is compliant with accessibility standards. Testing will complete with the submission of a compliance report.

Interoperability Testing

Testing to ensure that the product is able to coexist in a graceful way with common components and agents that are likely to be on the same logical server in common customer environments. This includes the ability to be installed and uninstalled without affecting other components as well as to be able to share available resources in an efficient way.

Securability Testing

There are several types of security-testing methodologies to be used. Vulnerability and security static code analysis, penetration testing, ethical hacking, and risk assessment are among key techniques that are used by most enterprise companies. This is to ensure that the product/component undergoes proper security and risk analysis to document vulnerabilities and formulate an appropriate remediation plan.

Securability testing is no longer considered as an afterthought and should be integrated into the code development cycle. Securability vulnerabilities should be prioritized and addressed along the way.

The way I often describe the importance of addressing vulnerabilities throughout the release lifecycle is as if you have used building blocks to beautifully architect a pyramid. If, after completing the pyramid, you realize that an incorrect block was used at the base and you try to replace it, the entire structure will get impacted and possibly destroyed. Testing along the way, identifying issues, and addressing them as they surface will save money.

Localizability Testing

Localizability consists of internationalization (i18n) and localization (l10n) testing. Once the content is translated, it is important to do content verification to ensure material is properly translated as per the language and culture.

Internationalization Readiness Testing

Testing that verifies that the component/feature, and in general the product as a whole, is properly internationalized so that it can be quickly and cost-effectively localized into any language.

Testing should include pseudo-localization tests that you intend to carry out to ensure your product meets the i18n requirements.[2]

Localization Testing

Testing that verifies that the translated material is linguistically correct and appropriate and that the localized product/component can be installed and looks and behaves as expected on US-English and localized environments (operating system, browser, database, third-party, and underlying technologies). While the focus is mainly on the web UI, it is important to also plan for translation of the product documentation, online help, command-line interface, log files, and so forth.

---

[2]https://www.youtube.com/watch?v=iWTs3PP12CO

Supportability Testing

Testing that ensures your product implements a known and consistent set of capabilities to enable customers to effectively consume products throughout the deployment lifecycle. For example, providing meaningful error/warning messages will allow customers and the Support department to resolve issues faster.

A great supportability consideration is to incorporate telemetry or a Call Home feature. That allows for faster diagnosis and often leads to improvements and solving customers' problems before they notice the issue—a great way to improve customer satisfaction!

Upgradability Testing

Testing that ensures your product can be upgraded to the new version of the release without a large investment of effort/hardware by the customer.

Base products and supported customizations should be able to be upgraded within predefined timeframes (this timeframe needs to be discussed and agreed upon during release planning).

Usability Testing

Testing of the application to ensure that the intended users of a system can carry out their tasks efficiently, effectively, and satisfactorily. Usability testing is carried out pre-release so that any significant issues are identified as well as to validate the application at a logical iteration boundary for new features.

Performance and Scalability Testing

Testing to ensure that system behaviour is as desired during normal load and determines the upper limit of allowed transactions or computations at the product level. This includes the scalability-testing approaches for various test levels of the product. For example, testing that checks program behavior during intense peaks of activity, or by printing 1,000 documents at once or opening the maximum number of files. It is important, however, to establish proper and acceptable limits in advance. With certain applications and without any such limits, the system eventually fails. It is better to relax the limits as customer use cases are better understood, if needed.

Evolution of Testing Over Time

While the preceding set of guidelines, types of testing, planning, and so forth will be relevant for many years to come, development departments should always stay current with new emerging technologies to continuously update and adjust their test strategy. In recent years, the following mentioned trends and technologies have gained a lot of publicity. I would like to make sure that I draw your attention to these specific areas and encourage you and your team to keep a close eye on how they could possibly change the landscape of your testing strategy. Some have started to influence the space more than others.

Internet of Things (IoT)

As great as it may sound, the world of connected devices and the integration nightmare that comes with it will bring interesting challenges to deal with. As an example, vulnerabilities resulting from connected products will create many additional dimensions to consider in your test strategy.

Big Data

Clients and users collect and upload terabytes of data on various platforms. Careful consideration for testing with a massive amount of data needs to be made for better alignment with the customer-like environment. Keep in mind that it is not always possible to build an exact customer's environment for internal validation, but getting to as close to customer's configuration as possible is the objective here.

Mobile Users and Test Automation

More and more customers demand mobile support for their applications. Testing mobile applications and considering unique angles with respect to the number of regular software updates and types of devices deserve their own test strategy and planning.

API and Microservice

Microservices and emphasis on a rich API-based design fit well with the Agile discipline and methodologies. There are many differences as compared to the traditional testing of the whole system in a waterfall approach. Getting bits and pieces available to test will require better planning, coordination, and optimization of the environment used. Each independent service will have to be tested separately and then as part of an interconnected structure. The best approach here is to go back to the Test Pyramid basics and start with a strong unit-test strategy followed by functional, integration, and E2E testing, which we have already talked about.

Adoption of Open Source Tools

Open source tools have been popular in many industries for testing their applications. The days where one tool was used to test the entire application are gone. With optimization that determines which open source tool to use for what layer of testing you can reduce costs and improve productivity.

AI and Machine Learning

Many organizations have been able to streamline their testing and coverage at all levels by leveraging various sources of data that are available to them. Such data reside in teams' existing test-case management and defect-reporting systems (logging, resolution details, and regression info), along with their source-code repository data. Utilizing such data can help identify particular heat-map and problem areas in the product. Historical data is a treasure that can be used to train AI algorithms to measure risk, classify defects, and predict delivery of solutions to customers.

Crowdsource Testing

This is becoming more and more popular, especially with constant budget pressure. Not being able to hire internal or contract resources to do thorough exploratory testing has driven some organizations to take this approach. The biggest challenge here is the security concerns that exist and need to be dealt with.

Self-Reflection Questions

- Why is it important to have a test strategy story for every applicable feature?

- Who should participate in a test-strategy discussion meeting? When is the best time to discuss test strategy for new features and program increments?

- Do you follow a layered testing approach in your organization?

- Where should the majority of testing focus be directed–at the unit test or higher up in the layered Test Pyramid?

- What is abilities testing?

- How could AI, big data, crowdsourcing, and telemetry impact the future of testing?

Quality Excellence Journey

Start with a Proof of Concept

At this point, you have seen examples of quality transformations happening within teams and organizations. We have also created a framework for such efforts and discussed the need to start with a Quality Integral Map and create a VSEM (Vision, Strategy, Execution, Measurement) to lead you through your journey.

When you begin any major transformation project that involves a large enterprise and requires changes in the culture, it is important to define your VSEM first, but be sure to perform a proof of concept (PoC) before you get to wider adoption at a larger scale. In this chapter, I have chosen a specific experience to share with you where the culture of quality changed significantly. The steps that we followed and the results that we achieved resonated very positively with customers and made a significant impact on our NPS scores, which ultimately impacted revenue. We were then able to use the learnings to scale at a much bigger level across the entire enterprise!

© CA 2019

N. Nader-Rezvani, *An Executive's Guide to Software Quality in an Agile Organization*,
https://doi.org/10.1007/978-1-4842-3751-9_8

Validate Quality Framework Effectiveness

During the early stages of an enterprise transformation discussion, we realized that it was more effective to start with one product team as an early adopter of the new process. This would allow us to truly anticipate and validate the challenges that other product teams and larger departments would run into along the transformation journey.

It was important to validate the new processes, which included an effective implementation of the quality framework; work closely with teams to highlight their challenges; and handhold them throughout the initial stages of the transformation. This PoC experience provided insight into potential challenges and paved the way for other teams that needed to adopt the same blueprint for their transformation.

A series of meetings was held with the executive leadership team to choose a product that was strategic and had the most appetite for change and need for quality improvement. After a couple of weeks considering key factors such as revenue, current NPS score, and Agile maturity, we had a direction. The product we chose was strategic and could certainly use quality improvements in all defined pillars of quality!

While the entire business unit was already on board with the need to put focus on product quality, the "how" part was not fully understood.

The entire organization had already adopted the five NQPs (Navid's Quality Pillars):

- People and Agile Processes
- Code Quality
- DevOps and Development Productivity
- Abilities such as Upgradability, Securability, Supportability, etc.
- Voice of the Customer in All Phases of Product Development

The next steps that were taken are summarized here:

- Product X was chosen as the focused product area for which to improve quality.
- Figure 8-1 shows an example of NPS comments breakdown for product X.

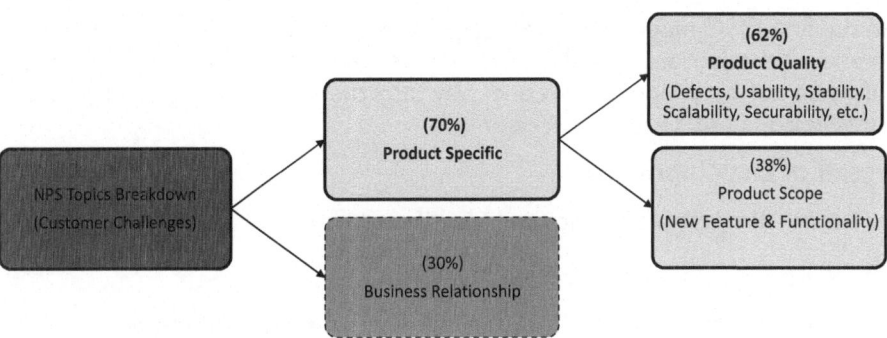

Figure 8-1. Example of NPS customer comments breakdown for a product line

- Series of NPS comments where product quality was highlighted as a challenge were reviewed. Such quality-related comments represented over 60 percent of the total in the product section. It was hard to argue with real data!

- Created awareness and sense of urgency for special quality focus. Understanding that quality is not JUST about defects was an important message to reiterate.

- Established a cross-functional Quality Steering Committee (QSC) to focus on the defined NQPs, created a baseline, identified owners for each area, put continuous focus on identifying gaps, and created a plan to execute against.

- Members of the QSC included:
    - Support Leader
    - DevOps Leader
    - PM Leader
    - Development Leader
    - Sustaining Leader (separate triage sustaining, L2, team existed for this product)
    - Test Architect
    - Dev Architect
    - Quality Advocate Leader
    - Sales and Services (in advisory roles)

In the first QSC meeting, several suggestions were made. First, start with who the key contributors would be and ensure they fully understand the impact of what will be proposed. Second, play into the Quality Integral Map! Some specific comments are discussed next.

Head of Development:

- Review set metrics and identify next steps

Development Architect:

- Define KPIs to track against and continuously inspect and validate results to ensure proper KPIs are chosen to track.

- Come up with a reasonable list of items to focus on and be ok with an imperfect process while on this journey, as long as we are making progress against our set interim goals.

Head of Support:

- Understand specific initiatives taken on by the product team to drive set metrics and then track progress against them in our dashboard.

- Identify roadblocks, review customers' hot spots, and discuss how to go about resolving them.

- Have specific plans and accountability across the product team to address hot spots reported by customers.

Head of Product Management:

- Define what success represents in each of the areas identified, discuss what actions we are going to take against each area, and take that material and share with our constituents (i.e., Sales).

- Need to be declaratively specific on what *good* means and how we make progress in each of the areas.

- Track leading and trailing indicators to adjust our plans if needed.

QA Architect:

- Clearly define what dimension of quality we are focusing on and what the specific measurements will be against set goals.

- Pick top few items to go after instead of a broad set.

- Consider team's bandwidth and plan accordingly.

- Define clear next steps with owners.

- Take each of the defined pillars and spend time

  - defining what success looks like;

  - identifying the key pain points; and

  - defining what the ultimate goal is and who is responsible.

It was important to get input from all cross-functional team members and ensure there was alignment to move forward, in addition to having a commitment from the executive leadership team. We took everyone's input into consideration and met weekly to do exactly what was recommended:

- Identified key quality pain points.

- Identified key stakeholders and contributors and looked at quality challenges from their lenses.

- Assessed current state of the product team in each of the five NQPs.

- Created a roadmap with specific objectives and timeline for continuous improvement.

- Defined what success looked like at each milestone.

- Assigned owners for each area that was voted to have highest priority.

- Defined success metrics.

- Tracked progress against set goals.

It was important to have a regular cadence for those meetings, at which all steering committee members would come together and update the team on their action items. Here are some specific outcomes after a few such weekly meetings. In the meantime, there was communication with the entire product team to get feedback and ensure buy-in at all levels:

- A shared location for the product team was identified to capture weekly progress and updates.

- Product management was instrumental in adding key quality-impacting factors into the product backlog and prioritizing them accordingly.

- Transparency, accountability, and acknowledgment of the problem on hand significantly helped clarify objectives and plan of action.

- Recommendation for additional investment was made to the Engineering/PM/senior leadership to accelerate certain key initiatives.

- A separate capacity and budget were approved to focus on the identified quality-impacting technical debt items. As an example, after creating a solid automation framework, we did an analysis to show that it was more effective to hire contractors with a solid working agreement and SLA than to add the task of automating high-priority regression test cases to teams' backlog. This outsourced project was funded and managed separately, but all scrum teams were engaged and able to enjoy the benefits. A win-win situation for all!

- Close working relationship between Engineering and Support was established. High-priority cases coming to Support were reviewed as a team, and areas of improvements were identified. Teams then reviewed design architecture, test case and automation details, and documentation to help reduce future reported customer issues in such areas. RCCA (Root Cause and Corrective Action) became part of the culture.

- Additional automated test cases were enjoyed by the product scrum teams and eliminated the need to manually execute tests, hence reducing the hardening phase and the back end of the release cycle.

- Performed a value-stream analysis on the build process. It was highlighted that builds were not continuing as soon as a problem surfaced. Significantly improved developers' productivity by parallelizing build process and streamlining platform support. Allowing the errors to be logged and the remainder of the build process to continue allowed for better debugging and reduced downtime.

- Engaged customers via an established validation program to ensure relevant solutions were being built by the product team.

- Reduced the hardening phase (tail end of the release) by more than 50 percent initially and improved automation coverage by 60 percent.

- Significantly reduced customer-issues backlog by allocating ongoing team capacity to address issues.

- Reviewed over 4,000 customer cases and collaborated with Sales/Services/Support to identify relevant Tier I reference architectures to focus on during development cycle. While all possible configurations were reviewed to be supported, only five were selected for in-depth analysis and testing.

- Identified upgrade as a challenge, collaborated with Support and Services, and initiated an upgrade pilot program with three customers. This gave a strong message to customers that we truly cared about their feedback on upgrade challenges and allowed us to improve our upgrade tools and documentation and address unique product issues that were not identified internally. We had engineers onsite to handhold the customer through their upgrade process, took notes of challenges, and ensured those areas were addressed by the product team. The engagement resulted in a services contract and strengthened relationship with customers.

- Standardized our hot fix, patch, service packs, and minor releases. As a result of reviewing and establishing regular cadence on our service packs, we reduced the need to have frequent hot fixes and allowed the customers to plan for their upgrade accordingly.

- Leveraged an internal customer-like environment to focus on upgrades in an integrated environment to weed out key issues before the release date.

- Hired a third-party vendor to do performance benchmarking against our competition. The benchmarking data was significant and it generated a lot of interest from the field. This was needed to win deals but didn't tie down internal resources to impact other high-priority items.

The following are the results that were achieved in less than 18 months by implementing the preceding processes. Regular meetings with the QSC members and input from the scrum teams allowed for continuous process improvement.

- Improved MTTR (Mean Time To Resolution) by 50 percent via

  - focused training for support engineers to reduce MTTR for LI;

  - prioritized issues for Sustaining L2 team to address and achieved a great collaboration among the two organizations to define clear processes; and

- reported on total MTTR to focus on L1+L2 as customers did not differentiate where the internal bottleneck was.

- Reduced number of customer escalations by more than 90 percent via

  - weekly review of early warnings and

  - regular support engagement for proper prioritization.

- Increased test automation coverage to 60 percent by

  - leveraging support data and

  - elevating test-strategy discussion at the release level.

- Improved PSM by greater than 90 percent by

  - creating awareness on total possible combination of greater than 4 million and

  - utilizing Support, Sales, and Services data to identify a handful of certified configurations to focus on.

- Improved hardening phase by 50 percent by

  - using a better test strategy that was change based;

  - providing training on required testing; and

  - leveraging automation.

- NPS improved by greater than 200 percent in one year because

  - product quality improvements resonated with customers;

  - some even got excited to know that we had a quality framework; and,

  - more importantly, we gained the trust of many customers that had stated previously that we were not serious about product quality and had become numb to it!

The mindset started to shift, and quality was no longer being viewed as someone else's responsibility or an element to slow product teams down. Process innovation became part of the culture. Teams started to realize the benefits of focusing on specific quality-impacting factors and truly enjoyed the opportunity to make a difference and change customers' perception. We had happier employees and happier customers! Of course, with that came additional revenue. More important, other product teams started to pay attention to what this particular product team was able to accomplish. This was what we needed to better promote the vision of quality across the enterprise!

Practical Guidelines to Remember

It is essential to remember that change is difficult and transformation is a tough process to walk through. Sometimes teams get overwhelmed with a large list of improvements, get discouraged, and delay the process for "later." Well, "later" may never arrive, and teams will continue to struggle with known challenges. In the preceding example, the initiative took time, and effort from the entire organization was needed. If we didn't have commitment and a framework to help prioritize what needed to be focused on first, it wouldn't have worked.

There are several elements to keep in mind while going through an extremely difficult quality-improvement journey. Focusing on the following few items will help ease the pain.

Be Open to Taking Risks If You Believe in the Cause

When you are starting on a journey that requires changes that impact the culture, you may not have all the answers or a full guarantee that the approach will work. At some point, you need to be ready to begin and maybe even put your reputation at risk if you truly believe in the cause. I have done that a good number of times!

Don't Boil the Ocean

Ensure you have a master plan/blueprint/framework and assess your current state against it. Consider the top one or two items from each category, prioritize, and commit to those in a meaningful schedule.

Prioritize and Break Down Challenges to Solve the Most Critical Items

Every problem can be broken down into small chunks to be tackled. If we don't try to break them down, it overwhelms the team and demotivates them to the point that it is easier to give up than find a solution.

Identify Business Value of Quality Initiative

For business leaders who are driven by revenue and outcome, it is important to be able to articulate the ROI for any initiative that you are asking them to fund. Identify the most significant change required and translate it into business-impact dollars This is particularly critical if they have lost their trust in the ability of the team to deliver value on time.

Over-communicate Objectives

Once agreements are there to launch an initiative, communicate at all levels, generate excitement, and be sure to consider the Quality Integral Map; you must also view the world from various lenses. Also, it helps to articulate the objectives in a way that exposes the "what is in it" for everyone involved: team members, organization as a whole, and customers. When everyone is in alignment with respect to objectives and timelines, a great sense of teamwork and collaboration will be observed at all levels.

Paint a Picture of What Success Looks Like

Teams need to know what success looks like at every milestone and when they will be done with one initiative so they can start on the next. Remember, milestones should be considered as stepping stones in the quality journey. Clearly defining what the scope is and what is not included will provide a great sense of clarity for all and will reduce confusion and frustration.

Break Down Team/Function Silos

Once a common objective is communicated and only teams are recognized and not individual heroes, there is a huge incentive to work together rather than get ahead of others. It is important to clarify and continuously promote the value of a team over individualism.

Assess Team's Skills, Train, and Attract New Talent

Ensuring we have the right people on the bus is important. Defining critical roles and skills and assessing existing team members will allow for identifying gaps and closing them faster to help achieve objectives efficiently.

Set Goals, Measure, Evaluate, Then Take Action

Articulating up front what success looks like, what outcomes the team should be looking for, and what metrics are going to be collected to evaluate progress will make a huge difference in helping the team achieve their goals and take proper action.

Keep the Engine Going While Making Improvements; Do No Harm

Everyone should understand that it likely took many years to build up the quality technical debt; therefore, it is not possible to make it magically disappear overnight no matter how much effort you put in. The business cannot come to a halt so teams can catch up on years of technical debt. However, careful planning and proper prioritization, dedicated bandwidth, commitment from teams and leadership, and awareness to avoid building new technical debt will be the most effective process to follow.

Once a social agreement is established to go on this journey, eliminating *new* technical debt should be listed as the highest priority. This means that while you may not be able to immediately attend to *existing* technical debt, at least you are not adding new ones to the list. This comes at a cost and requires proper training, planning, and commitment, which must be clearly communicated to the entire organization.

A bit of great advice for developers is to always try to leave the code somewhat cleaner than the state in which it was originally found. For example, if you are fixing a customer issue and notice some coding best practices being violated in the same area, try to fix that as well. Every little bit helps and will save time in the future. An example that may resonate with you is when a surgeon is operating on a patient for a specific treatment and has already cut him open, she might fix another adjacent area if she notices an issue in order to avoid another future surgery!

Recognize Team's Effort Along the Journey

Once standard processes are in place, it is important to empower teams to take calculated risks and track their progress, as follows:

- Market and showcase progress.
- Never plan for maximum capacity of teams per release to allow for uncertainties and variability.

- Celebrate wins (i.e., meeting commitment versus planned story points for the first time, first found bug in new automation suite, etc.).

- Focus on results and outcomes rather than efforts.

- Be open to new ways of solving problems.

In summary, before operationalizing any major changes at the enterprise level, it is critical to do a PoC at a product team and organization level. That will allow challenges to be dealt with at a smaller scale and ensure scalability when processes are implemented at a much higher scale in enterprise. Quality transformation is difficult and can take a long time. Built-in quality is expected in Agile. Quality is a journey and a mindset. You can't expect to be done with quality, as it is a long, continuous improvement process. It takes a whole village to walk through this journey—not a selected function!

Self-Reflection Questions

- Why is it important to design a Proof of Concept before operationalizing an initiative across the entire enterprise?

- What were some key elements responsible for a successful transformation in the PoC covered in the chapter?

- What are some initiatives that you would like to operationalize in your organization?

- How would you go about designing a PoC and product-selection process to validate your new initiative?

- Why is it important to establish a steering committee for new transformation initiatives?

- Why is it important to communicate the ROI on new initiatives for the business leaders?

- What are some key guidelines for teams and leaders to remember when they embark on their quality-improvement journey?

- What is the definition of NPS? Why is it important to improve NPS?

Quality at Scale

Engrave Culture of Quality in an Enterprise

In earlier chapters, I shared examples of the quality continuous-improvement journey at the product-team level to provide tangible results. I also shared examples of such transformations at a business-unit level (consisting of many product teams), and now we will turn our attention to such initiatives at the enterprise level. Extending a similar journey and cultural changes across the enterprise is much harder as it requires extreme levels of coordination and steering. Figure 9-1 shows an example of an enterprise organizational setup.

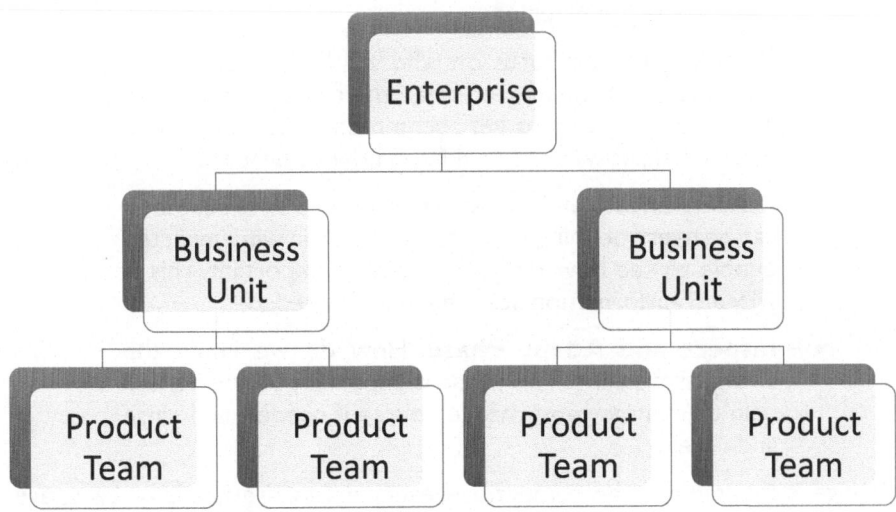

Figure 9-1. Enterprise organizational setup

© CA 2019

N. Nader-Rezvani, *An Executive's Guide to Software Quality in an Agile Organization*, https://doi.org/10.1007/978-1-4842-3751-9_9

Just to add to the complexity, some enterprises may need to adapt to acquisitions and global outsourcing that inevitably raise walls between teams, introduce different tools and processes, and redirect attention to short-term priorities that are not consistent with the business case. To ensure quality has appropriate representation in business discussions, it is important to create a transparent culture, acknowledge challenges with the ever-changing environment, promote standard definitions, and reinforce business metrics that are impacted by product quality.

One of the key principles of Agile is the ability to respond to change rather than simply following a set plan. Some leaders get nervous with this, as they immediately think portfolio planning is moot in Agile. It is actually quite the opposite. Agility elevates the need and importance of the portfolio-planning and decision-making processes. In fact, maintaining alignment through evolution and change by focusing on effective approaches in portfolio planning and prioritization is a powerful mechanism for Agile leaders.

Critical Stages of Change

Appreciating the critical stages of change is always helpful in guiding organizations to stay focused despite roadblocks and uncertainties:

- **Discovery Phase:** Fully invest in what problem we are solving and understand what the impact of change will be. This is what we referred to earlier when discussing Quality Integral Mapping.

- **Deciding Phase:** Focus on who will be impacted, what the scope is of the impact, when the change is expected, and how it is going to get accomplished (focus on who, what, when, how), then decide on how to proceed.

- **Implementation Phase:** When change is executed, it can be overwhelming. Continuous check-in with impacted people to see how things are going is important. This is why a transformation steering team is needed.

- **Inspect and Adapt Phase:** How do we know the change is working? This phase is important because it will help us manage gaps, change course if needed, and rinse and repeat.

Change is inevitable. To be competitive, every enterprise needs to be aware, be agile, adapt, and react fast. Change is hard, but if we plan, communicate, collaborate, lead effectively, under promise, and over deliver, we can expect a successful but difficult change journey!

This section will provide an overview of a quality-transformation initiative at an organization with over 3,500 product team members. The results that the teams achieved in one year were enough to convince everyone at the company that this journey needed to be further fueled and continued.

Background

In this particular company, there were many quality challenges, and a clear vision and strategy was desperately needed to align everyone at all levels. There were many clues left by customers that helped us get to the initial phase of understanding what problem we needed to prioritize and solve first. The enterprise customers were not shy about letting us know via NPS feedback or escalation calls about their disappointment with the overall quality of our products. The issues spanned across multiple pillars of quality:

- Complexity of upgrades and inconsistent release and service-pack schedules

- Downtime for SaaS products that impacted their production

- Integration challenges of our various products that customers owned

- Product defects in new features and regression in existing releases; a significant number of escalations spoke to this point

- Unacceptable turnaround time on reported issues; MTTR (Mean Time to Resolution) high numbers

- Insufficient or inaccurate documentation

All business units had gone through Agile and SAFe training and were practicing the disciplines at different levels of maturity, but at least every product team in every business unit was familiar with the Agile principles. While product teams had marched into the Agile world, they were still struggling with delivering value to customers in a timely manner and with high quality. It seemed as though they were getting numb to the quality challenges that were being brought up by customers.

Many departments came together, including Support, to help put a spotlight on the problem at hand. Even at the CEO level, the focus on product quality gained a lot of attention. The head of all product teams was tasked to "fix" the product-quality challenges and incorporate a culture of quality at the company level. One of the senior members directly reporting to him was appointed to be the quality "czar." His responsibility was to take the entire product team through a successful quality transformation and delight customers. He quickly established a group of quality-passionate advisors to determine the scope and come up with a plan. Together, they crafted their mission and rules of engagement as follows:

Mission:

- We are dedicated to a relentless pursuit of incrementally increasing product quality to improve customer outcomes.

- With customer engagement as a foundation, we will drive ideal customer outcomes by harmonizing product quality with the value it delivers.

- Quality is our guiding compass from ideation to customer validation and engagement to ensure we deliver uncommon product value that helps our customers attain their desired outcomes.

Transparency as a key rule of engagement:

- Information regarding this quality initiative was posted on an internal page and made available to the entire company. Information was also shared as part of the quality status report delivered to the CEO, GMs, and SVPs of Product Development.

- This program was structured to ensure accountability and transparency into the components of the program and the progress each business unit was making.

A transformation of this magnitude was not an easy task. Coordination at all levels internally and collaboration with customers externally were needed to make this a successful journey. Another important factor was to ensure that this quality program was established as an enabler and not as a policing function. Each business unit was asked to internalize quality-impacting factors and come up with their own quality targets and remediation plans.

Internal and Independent Audit

After each business unit performed some levels of assessment and considered the Quality Integral Map, it became clear that having an independent internal audit (IA) team to validate the performed assessments would be a good next step. The IA team had the responsibility of assessing and reporting on quality metrics across the product team department. However, after reviewing the standard assessment questionnaire that the IA team was intending to use, it became obvious that they were mainly reflecting a waterfall product-development approach. The quality advisors helped rewrite the audit details, identified key quality metrics, and selected a handful of strategic products to perform the quality audit for.

These questions were designed to help get visibility into the current state of quality across all business units and every product team. It was also an opportunity for the product teams to internalize key dimensions that influenced their overall quality and be able to thoroughly assess each specific area. The questionnaire was among the initial steps to help them plan short-term versus long-term initiatives that would allow the teams to continuously improve their overall product quality.

Based on the consolidated report from the IA team, the quality czar and his advisors were able to determine what common metrics they should select and set as a common standard across the company. Over time, and as teams gained higher quality maturity levels, an additional set of metrics were introduced, selected, and reported against.

The new set of questions used by the IA team shown in Figure 9-2 were based on the five NQPs (Navid's Quality Pillars) that were defined in earlier chapters.

Product Quality Topic Scorecard
• Describe how you ensure proper skills/roles are represented in your scrum teams.
• Describe how you measure code quality and ensure best software development processes are followed.
• Describe your DevOps process/tools and attention to the productivity of the team.
• Describe your focus on the foundational requirements of the product.
• Describe how you incorporate the voice of the customer in every aspect of your development process.
• Describe how your team distinguishes between Agile Acceptance and Done criteria.
• Describe your team's continuous quality-improvement activities.

Figure 9-2. Product quality independent audit questions

Maturity levels were assigned to each of the product teams as per the Internal Audit preceding questions:

1. Informal

2. Established

3. Repeatable

To no one's surprise, most products were initially hovering somewhere around the "Informal" level, which represented a red status and considered the audit for those products to have produced a failed result. The internal audit confirmed that there was no consistency across the portfolio of products around quality processes, standards, reporting, key risk indicators (KRIs), and key performance indicators (KPIs).

The initial reported results from the Internal Audit team were summarized as:

Product-Quality Framework:

An Agile-aligned product-quality framework that delineates common product-quality topics and tasks for the product-development teams has not been consistently adopted.

Product-Quality Tracking:

Product-development teams do not use consistent product backlog category names to facilitate management visibility into developer activities specifically designed to address product-quality topics.

Product-Quality Reporting:

Standard product-quality reporting aligned with the product-quality framework does not exist.

The preceding findings were shared in the CEO town hall, where a commitment was voiced to put the necessary focus and investment in achieving a sustainable passing grade when future Internal Audits were to be conducted. This is when the entire company got behind this initiative and the quality czar took things to the next level.

Aligning All Functions Around Quality, Not Just the Product Teams

In this company, there was another initiative around lifecycle management that focused on understanding challenges related to upgrading to later versions of the products. In fact, a new organization was created to focus solely on "lifecycle management." As we discussed earlier, upgradability is one of the key abilities and a key pillar of quality.

The Lifecycle Management team's charter was to connect with customers to reduce their attrition, ensure our software was not just shelfware, understand upgrade challenges, and work with the product teams to reduce complexity and help customers gain value from our solution. Ultimately, the objective was to ensure our customers landed, adapted, expanded, and renewed our solution.

This initiative was critical because it provided insight into not only the customer versioning info, but also why they weren't at the latest versions. That info was then fed back to the product team with the goal of ultimately making the upgrade an uneventful process. Keep in mind that the chance of a customer staying with the vendor if they are current with the software version is much higher than if they are not current.

In parallel, the Support department started a new initiative around the customer journey to help highlight the vast opportunity that existed to attend to customers' needs. This exercise highlighted the following key items:

- We think of our customers more as companies with a bunch of executives rather than as users!

- We often value new features and functions instead of focusing on delivering value and ease of use for customers.

- We focus more on acquiring customers and less on their success, especially after the deal is closed.

A Customer Promise shown in Figure 9-3 was put together and shared with the entire company. Bringing in the voice of the customer and putting them at the center was a key dimension in quality and improving NPS that ultimately impacted revenue in a positive way.

The Customer Promise

We consistently deliver a superior experience by putting your organization at the center of all that we do. The ultimate measure of our success is through your success and earning your trust as a strategic partner.

Invest in Long-Term Relationship	Deliver Innovative Business Outcomes	Committed to Each Customer's Success
• Take time to understand customer's needs • Understand how products are used by customer • Maintain our engagement after initial sales	• Deliver products that solve relevant problems for customer • Work with customer to bring leading-edge technology • Simplify path to customer value	• #1 priority is to make customer successful • We deliver against our promise • We engage with customers until they realize their business outcome

Figure 9-3. Enterprise Customer Promise

So, all stars were aligned around getting this important initiative under way. The central tools team had created a very thorough DevOps/Productivity Tools maturity model. They had also identified a tiger team to educate teams in the key area of tools and other productivity-enhancer areas. That service was initially made available to the strategic products in the overall portfolio, but over time it was made available to all teams.

The recommendation from the advisory board was to expand the DevOps maturity model and include all other pillars of quality to get to a holistic quality maturity model. Figure 9-4 shows how the quality maturity model evolved over time at the enterprise.

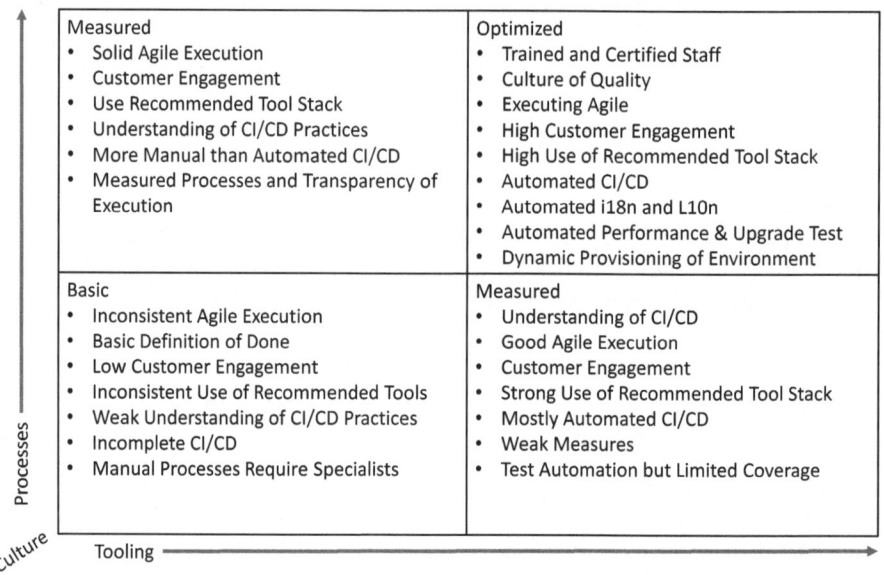

Measured	Optimized
• Solid Agile Execution • Customer Engagement • Use Recommended Tool Stack • Understanding of CI/CD Practices • More Manual than Automated CI/CD • Measured Processes and Transparency of Execution	• Trained and Certified Staff • Culture of Quality • Executing Agile • High Customer Engagement • High Use of Recommended Tool Stack • Automated CI/CD • Automated i18n and L10n • Automated Performance & Upgrade Test • Dynamic Provisioning of Environment
Basic	Measured
• Inconsistent Agile Execution • Basic Definition of Done • Low Customer Engagement • Inconsistent Use of Recommended Tools • Weak Understanding of CI/CD Practices • Incomplete CI/CD • Manual Processes Require Specialists	• Understanding of CI/CD • Good Agile Execution • Customer Engagement • Strong Use of Recommended Tool Stack • Mostly Automated CI/CD • Weak Measures • Test Automation but Limited Coverage

Processes / Culture / Tooling

Figure 9-4. Enterprise quality maturity model

An assessment was done for different products based on the preceding model and was provided to all teams to use for their short-term and long-term focus on quality.

Another key focus for the central tools team was to integrate the toolchain that existed. Without integration among different tools (i.e., customer defect reporting, internal defect reporting, test case management, CI/CD tools) and with no automated flow of artifacts among them, there would be little consistent reporting or traceability among those tools. Data consistency is key for reviewing trends and eventually using the historical data in artificial intelligence and machine learning to continuously improve.

A grassroots initiative was also kicked off to get quality-passionate individuals to come together on a weekly basis to focus on various aspects of quality, collaborate, and define standard approaches to be adopted by all teams to enhance quality and shift left.

This quality special interest group (SIG) focused on creating a standard early-release warning dashboard, a common set of DoD/DoR, internal defect severity definition standards, test strategy story template, and productivity tools. The results were made available to all product teams across the company. This was particularly important at this company due to the quality process variations that existed among various business units. Many acquisitions were responsible for such variations. This SIG was also responsible for recommending the next meaningful set of metrics to use across the enterprise as the departments moved up the quality maturity model.

Building a Quality Champion Change Agent Team

The next step was to build a cross-functional team of quality champions that represented each of the business units in the entire company. Every general manager was asked to assign a senior member of her/his department to participate in weekly quality-transformation champion meetings and contribute to the success of the enterprise quality. The business-unit champions had accountability for the business-unit team's execution of the program. Identifying members and establishing this important steering committee was a significant milestone for this initiative!

There was a need to educate the members and focus on the "why" for establishing such a steering committee. Remember, quality had not been a major focus for some teams. Reinforcing business metrics for quality was needed to ensure that at every stage, quality had appropriate representation in the business discussions. The user-journey initiative by the Support department and the Lifecycle Management team provided excellent detailed info on how product quality was impacting the renewal rate and hurting revenue.

Every business unit was consulted on their view of important metrics to capture for their product teams. Considering the enterprise quality maturity level, it was agreed upon that selecting a small set of critical business-driver metrics would be more valuable initially than using a broad set of metrics. Feedback from each of the business-unit leaders and quality champions on which problems to go after first revealed two specific metrics that directly impacted business metrics:

- **Reducing MTTR** – This was a common challenge across the board:
  - Customer opens an issue with support—clock starts
  - Support determines this to be a high-priority defect and engages development engineers

- Engineering triages the issue and provides Support with a resolution

- Support provides the resolution to the customer— MTTR clock stops

- **Reducing number of escaped defects to the customers**

  - Measure of the effectiveness of our pre-release quality-assurance process, including skills and software-development good practices, tooling and automation, abilities, and customer validation

  - Needed to remove customers as our extended QA arm!

The preceding two items became a standard set of metrics to track on a weekly basis for the first three quarters. This required a set of integrated tools to aid in extracting such data automatically, but it was well worth the effort. The central tools team did a fantastic job of assisting teams in collecting such metrics. Although this initially seemed like a metric and numbering exercise, it promoted good behavior and hygiene over time.

Each business unit assessed their current state and set specific goals to reduce their MTTR and escaped defects by a certain percentage point. If the reported results were above the agreed-upon numbers, a red status was assigned to that product team and actions were taken with specific ETAs to get back on track. Over time, a more sophisticated tool was made available to predict where each team's metrics would reside by the end of each quarter. Empowering the team to make a business decision on what portion of their investment to dedicate to quality initiatives versus new features resonated with the GMs and other business leaders.

This initiative gained a lot of attention. Teams started to look at key contributing factors that influenced the set metrics. The team of quality-passionate members in the quality special interest group spent many hours identifying which knobs needed to be turned to get better quality results. Here are specific areas that were identified for the escaped defect metric:

- Code coverage
- Test coverage
- Automation strategy at all levels
- Following Agile practices to close defects earlier
- Integration of automation tools in CI/CD
- Documentation review

- Access to customer-like environment, use cases, and data

- Upgrade and scalability focus

- Training for the sustaining triage teams if applicable

- Dependencies on third-party software

- Integration and interoperability focus

- Following coding standard practices and promoting extreme programing

- Solid root-cause analysis and corrective action

Clearly, investment in quality and attending to technical-debt reduction was in order. To get better visibility into the level of investment, every story or feature in the backlog related to quality initiatives was captured and reported on. The objective was to align the level of effort spent on quality initiatives with that spent on outcomes. Teams with high MTTR and escaped defects with no quality-investment stories/features in their backlog were flagged for a deeper review. The idea was to ensure awareness at all levels of the choices that product teams were making in regard to new features and continuous quality improvement.

The highly influential team of quality champions on the steering committee helped bridge the gap between corporate quality objectives and what actions were needed on each product team to build a culture of quality. As champions, their role was to learn the ins and outs of the quality initiative, listen to their team's concerns about any parts of the initiative, and help teams walk through their quality-transformation journey by removing obstacles and being present to provide support.

The following is a set of basic principles that were used as constant reminders for the teams to help establish a quality mindset in the departments:

- Focus on the customer and people first.

- Fail fast and learn from mistakes.

- Establish teams with collaborative and skilled people.

- Provide guidance and training to the leadership team to believe and support the change.

- Focus on creating a safe environment that allows for changing culture and mindset.

In these types of enterprise quality-transformation initiatives, creating visibility at the portfolio level by defining an epic to focus on quality is useful to help keep focus on the investment required across all product teams. Planning and delivering incremental quality improvements in every iteration/release and tracking such investments under the quality epic at the portfolio level provides visibility into the return on required investment. It will also help quality to get integrated in the culture of the enterprise.

Since quality improvement is a journey and teams will never be done with improving quality, creating a holistic quality epic will allow a quality-improvement roadmap to be created by teams and then executed against.

Tracking Quality Investment: Quality Epic

In every release, we want to ensure that overall quality is higher than in its predecessor. But remember: quality is not just limited to defects. Quality is perceived as the total customer experience, from the time they search online for a solution, all the way through their buyer's journey, installation, ease of use, expected functionality, support engagement, and upgrade experience. Often, the customer's experience in the preceding stages is reflected in the product-quality section of the NPS.

To continuously improve overall quality, it is important to create a quality blueprint for the product. It is expected that each product team will review the five NQPs (Navid's Quality Pillars), create a maturity model based on their current state, and prioritize the items that are critical to the success of their customers. Tracking such an investment by teams will provide higher visibility into the required level of focus and will allow for ROI calculations.

Identifying the following investment categories for every feature is a great way to provide the executive team with visibility into what the cost will be and the return on investing in areas that provide value to the customers:

- **Differentiator/Competitive/Create Revenue**: a feature that provides market-unique benefits to customers and maintains a competitive edge. It will generate new sales. These are items that "separate us from the pack."

- **Table Stakes**: a feature that is expected for any product in the market category. These are the minimum requirements to play or must haves that users expect.

- **Enabler**: a feature that establishes a capability that will support new functionality in future release(s). These are about architecture and infrastructure enhancements.

- **Protect Revenue and Reduce Costs**: a feature that will primarily drive renewals, upgrade sales, retain customers, lower cost of ownership, and improve maintenance— everything related to the holistic quality.

Here is an example of a quality epic that some organizations have used successfully to track their quality initiatives:

As a BU leader, I want to ensure quality is engraved in the DNA of the department and pay special attention to simplifying our offerings to reduce total cost of ownership.

1. Retain and attract talent to build a world-class development organization

Success Criteria:

- *Assess current talent pool of the department, both from Agile roles and technical expertise, and identify critical positions to fill on priority.*

- *Create a roadmap for training for individuals if needed and create a backlog item with specific training investments required.*

2. Simplify/modularize code architecture, improve code quality, ensure all modules (i.e., drivers, OS, TPSR (Third-Party Software Request), etc.) are up to date, there is adequate test coverage, and adhere to software development processes.

Success Criteria:

- *Utilize static and dynamic code-analysis tools to gather baseline.*

- *Create backlog items to address high-priority code violations, removal of unused code/duplicate, etc.*

- *Enforce coding standards and give testability of the code a high priority.*

- *Establish a clear DoR and DoD and adhere to it for story and iteration success (i.e., zero defects for new code and automation, code analysis and downstream impact, burn-down charts, test execution, code coverage, working software, and effective code review process are enforced).*

- *List of major components/modular/TPSRs that need updates are reviewed and backlog items are created to address as per priority.*

3. Drive Agile productivity tools and processes.

Success Criteria:

- *Baseline for DevOps capability model is understood and plans for key improvements are prioritized in the backlog (i.e., CI/CD). For example: Build time is reduced.*

- *Effective automation framework for CI/Functional/ Performance in place.*
- *Regression tests are prioritized for automation.*

4. Integrate abilities into your product cadence.

Success Criteria:

- *Backlog item is created to review all abilities, baseline scorecard for all abilities created and filled out, and gaps are identified.*
- *Key abilities impacting NPS and TCO are prioritized in the backlog (i.e., integration, upgrade, securability, etc.).*

5. Put customers at the center; bring voice of the customers into our product-development processes.

Success Criteria:

- *Backlog item is created to establish a baseline for the NPS highest-impacting factors:*
  - *Number of fixes required per customer per year, MTTR, customer defect backlog, customer hot spots, etc.*
  - *Prioritize agreed-upon NPS highest contributors in the backlog to address.*
  - *Create a baseline for the TCO highest-impacting factors (i.e., deployment, upgrade complexity, etc.).*
  - *Prioritize items in the backlog and address them.*
- *Customer Validation*
  - *Active customer participation in sprint reviews*
  - *Feature/charter approval*
  - *Tour de "product" with customers to learn their specific use cases*

By creating such an epic, teams started to have ongoing discussions about what more could be done in each of the pillars, broke the problems into smaller chunks, and added highest-priority items in every release to tackle. The need to have dedicated capacity to focus on continuous quality-improvement efforts became clear, and innovative ideas related to gaining higher productivity at all levels started to surface.

The role of the quality champions in this transformation was critical as they were constant reminders to the teams that customers expected releases to come with high quality. They might even forgive the occasional short delay in a release if it meant higher-quality features. The ultimate goal was of course to create value for customers with a velocity model where there was consistency in the release schedule.

I would like to emphasize the critical role the executive team and their support play in ensuring success when implementing a quality program. At this enterprise, each GM was encouraged to represent his or her product status regarding quality and the established metrics. The quality czar provided regular updates and focused on early warnings of any potential quality issues. He also engaged regularly with the product-line executive to ensure the executive and their team were aware of all statuses circulating to the senior executives or CEO. Accountability was felt at the top levels of the organization.

With all the focus and awareness around quality, the enterprise achieved amazing results. When such results were published after just three quarters of focusing on two basic metrics, it was obvious to the executive management team that ongoing investment was needed to continuously improve and delight customers.

In less than nine months, this company achieved the following amazing results for their strategic product lines:

- MTTR reduced by ~30%
- Defect backlog age down by ~15%
- Escaped defects reduced by greater than 10%

Creating clarity by identifying the following specific actions allowed various organizations to align and achieve a common goal of reducing MTTR and escaped defects:

- Standard quality process was established across the company by
  - assessing current state;
  - utilizing Agile processes to prioritize highest-impacting quality factors in the backlog for product teams; and
  - measuring and tracking quality investments via automated tools.
- Product quality audit conducted regularly by the IA team to allow for continuous quality improvement (rinse and repeat).

Efforts were measured against actual results!

What we learned through this journey was invaluable. At an enterprise, quality-improvement transformation is possible when quality has a seat at the table and a solid quality system is in place with commitment from all levels of the organization. It is true that everyone owns quality, but accountability needs to be discussed and internalized as well.

Acknowledging challenges around quality was needed for teams to get behind quality initiatives and for GMs to appoint representatives to help drive the culture of quality. Grassroots efforts were initiated to focus on areas that could be shifted to the left while keeping an eye on the defined lagging indicators/metrics. Establishing company-wide quality objectives and monitoring and reporting on set goals ensured continuous focus on improving quality.

As part of this exercise, it became apparent that while each team was at a different quality maturity level, it was important to select a small set of common metrics on which to be able to report at the executive-team level. As the teams gained higher levels of maturity, additional metrics were chosen and reported against.

In an enterprise, once a solid quality program is in place, it will help product and business leadership to balance customer needs (i.e., fixes & enhancements) and market and competitor forces with innovation. For example, if a product team is investing too much in sustaining one year, the quality metrics can help guide where that investment can be redirected. Understanding the right investment mix by performing an ongoing assessment is important so as to avoid product teams' falling into a status quo pattern. Successful organizations balance customer needs with new features, which is always a tough trade-off. If they have a solid quality system, it can help free up team members for innovation. It is critical to emphasize the need for strong executive support to ensure success!

Self-Reflection Questions

- Why is it more difficult to create a culture of quality at an enterprise level?

- Discuss the alignment among all functions in an enterprise and not just within the product teams.

- What are key steps to follow when you want to transform an enterprise and create a culture of quality?

- What is the importance of tracking quality investment for every product-team portfolio?

- What is the key role of a quality-champion team?

- Why was it important for the quality czar role to exist at an executive level?

- Discuss the importance of having an independent quality audit done across the enterprise and reporting on progress at the CEO town hall.

- Why were the two metrics chosen in the example effective?

- What is the definition of MTTR?

- How is escaped defect measured?

- What other metrics will be relevant once a team gains higher maturity?

Conclusion and Summary

I have covered many examples of how giving "quality" a seat at the table brings fruitful results. The goal was not to write a complete Agile quality playbook, but rather to share enough structured experienced-based examples to allow readers to understand how to create a relevant quality framework for their business. This would also aid them in changing the culture and mindset at all levels and in continuously improving. The examples covered mindset changes that were necessary to engrave quality in the DNA of a product team, a business unit, or an enterprise as a whole. In today's competitive market, putting customers at the center is no longer an option—it is a given.

Change is inevitable. To stay current and competitive in the market, companies need to adapt and continuously improve on their software development processes while attending to customer quality. You may have experienced and utilized certain practices and tools that were state of the art when they were first implemented. With the fast pace of technology, however, the very same practice that was once brand new is now obsolete and no longer as effective. The concept of inspecting and adapting to new changes in Agile allows for such challenges to be addressed along the journey and for companies to stay current and deliver value faster.

The concept of value-stream analysis is an effective one for evaluating the current state of any process and identifying areas that need to be optimized. Fewer handoffs along the way will allow for faster value delivery and will make it easier to build in quality. While you conduct the value-stream analysis,

© CA 2019
N. Nader-Rezvani, *An Executive's Guide to Software Quality in an Agile Organization*,
https://doi.org/10.1007/978-1-4842-3751-9_10

it is important to not limit input gathering from your internal teams, but rather to involve other cross-functional teams as well. Optimizing the system in its entirety will result in higher quality, happier customers, and faster value delivery.

We also discussed the importance of considering the Worldview concept and having a clear Quality Integral Map, knowing where you are, assessing options, and putting plans in place to address them. By performing such steps, a great visibility into where improvements are needed will emerge.

Keeping in mind that each feature and release is a new experience for customers is important. Getting their ongoing feedback will allow vendors to build the right thing. If the organization is not listening and is not willing to quickly adjust their course, they will lose their customers, no matter how loyal those customers were at the beginning.

When customers are the key focus for the organization, the final success criteria is whether they liked what was delivered. As a result, key questions that will help sharpen the organization's focus and provide a purpose for the work that teams do would be as follows:

- How much did the new feature impact revenue?

- How much deviation existed between planned versus actual delivery date for the feature?

- How widely is the feature getting adopted by customers? (Telemetry plays a big role here.)

- How much new business value was delivered with the new feature?

- Did it meet internal and external quality expectations?

Practicing and paying attention to what resonates with internal teams as well as with external customers will build a foundation for determining how to continuously identify key elements that matter. After internalizing this concept and practicing it, the process will require less effort, and the culture of quality will emerge. By adopting key Agile quality practices, some organizations have reported greater than 90 percent improvement in their productivity and overall quality.

Emphasizing the fact that quality and process improvement is a journey and not a destination should be part of every communication during the Agile quality-transformation process. Organizations need to internalize the journey, adopt key disciplines, and practice them. They need to continuously attend to those steps that can be done more efficiently and more effectively. Understanding that there is always room for improvement and planning to have an ongoing focus on such practices will allow the emergence of companies that can go from good to great!

It is not enough to invite a customer to one EoS demo or to integrate a new tool in the build process, or to hold a one-time bug squash sprint and be done with the quality initiative. If teams don't stay current with tools or customer feedback and don't continuously innovate on their processes, they won't stay competitive in the market. These changes will augment any efforts in achieving long-term growth and scalability while helping to guarantee viability and great success.

It is important to start shifting our mindset from thinking about projects to thinking about products and features. By definition, a project has a start and end time with deadlines. This doesn't align well with the concept of the continuous quality-improvement journey. Teams are expected to prioritize quality technical debt items in their backlog, iterate in short cycles, set a high quality bar, and continue to improve on an ongoing basis.

Facts about Quality Journey

The followings hold true about a quality journey:

- Takes time, as there is no silver bullet to help. You can't expect to be done overnight with addressing all the quality debt that was created over time. Quality is a journey and not a destination!

- Involves changing culture as one of key initial steps.

- Begins with a social contract with the team and executive leadership.

- Starts with an assessment of where the team, organization, and enterprise is and what success will look like; internalize Worldview and Quality Integral Map to guide you through the journey.

- Involves taking risks, having faith, and regularly inspecting to confirm, learn, and adapt accordingly.

- Requires an Agile mindset with proper training.

- Requires investment in elevating people at all levels in the organization.

- Requires investment in processes and tools (yes, this means spending money).

- Requires relentless effort, commitment, and accountability at all levels.

- Involves attracting new talent to enable the transformation; be prepared to lose people that cannot cope with change along the way.

- Has to be internalized to sustain. Pushing change on organizations without their seeing short-term results may not lead to a successful transformation.

- Requires effective communication at all levels to keep teams engaged, provide interim updates, realize short-term gains, and celebrate success along the way.

NQPs and Laws of Agile Quality

The Five NQPs (Navid's Quality Pillars) that I have described in this book should provide you with a strong blueprint regardless of where you are in your transformation journey. I have used the framework in multiple organizations to help educate the leadership team, scrum teams, and business owners. It has also helped with assessing the quality maturity of teams, organizations, and enterprises to help create a guiding principle on where to go next.

In conjunction with the NQPs, specific approaches were shared to address various items in each of the mentioned pillars. Such approaches can be summarized in a list of unique laws. My colleagues have often referred to them as Navid's Ten Laws of Agile Quality:

1. Law of Quality Cost Estimation & Benefits

2. Law of Baselining Quality Metrics

3. Law of Automation Economics

4. Law of Engaging Global Teams

5. Law of Effective Testing Coverage

6. Law of Horrific Reference Stack (PSM)

7. Law of Conservation of Long Tail or Hardening Phase

8. Law of Voice of the Customer and Tour de "Product"

9. Law of Continuous Learning (and Unlearning)

10. Law of Collaboration with Customer-Facing Organizations

It is important to keep in mind that certain approaches that worked in one organization may not *exactly* fit another. As I mentioned before, there is no single silver bullet that will work for every organization as they go through their Agile quality journey. The NQP and the Laws of Agile Quality will provide you with some guiding principles to use as you see fit.

Key Takeaways in Agile Quality Transformation

<u>**At the Team Level:**</u>

- Communicate the social contract at all levels.

- Ensure emphasis is put on outcomes and not solely on efforts.

- Have leaders be present, talk about the objectives, acknowledge challenges along the way, and help support the team.

- Create a clear vision, strategy, execution plan, and success measures and communicate what success looks like along the way.

- Do not try to boil the ocean; set achievable goals that are realistic.

- Prioritize and break down challenges to address.

- Assess against the Five NQPs and remember the Laws of Agile Quality:

    - Assess skills needed to succeed, retrain, and attract new talent to build a winning TEAM!

    - Select the highest critical quality-impacting factor that needs focus, make a compelling business case, and highlight expected savings in dollars for the proposed changes.

    - Create a quality roadmap for ongoing focus and future planning.

- Hire strong coaches with quality mindsets to help make your Agile quality transformation a success.

- Keep an eye on promoters and detractors of the change along the way.

- Create a safe environment where transparency and accountability are encouraged; questioning during the transformation journey is healthy. *Sometimes the emperor may just not be wearing any clothes!*

- Over-communicate your objectives, identify critical metrics to track progress against your goals, evaluate, and take action. Inspect and Adapt should be an integral part of the process.

- Keep the engines running (i.e., focus on the current release) and emphasize "Do No Harm" to avoid building new quality technical debt.

- Catch people following standard practices and promote such practices with the rest of the teams. This may require certain unlearning by the product team to take place. Remember that killing old habits could be difficult and constant reminders will be needed.

- Empower teams to self-organize and commit and be ready to take calculated risks!

- Make sure to market and showcase team's progress and celebrate their success!

At the Enterprise Level:

- Identify the business value of quality initiatives to gain traction.

- Ensure the executive team is on board and that there is an executive sponsor assigned to the initiative who is present and truly believes in such a journey.

- Establish a steering committee representing every department and ensure there is a social contract at all levels.

- Perform a value stream analysis from a 360-degree view to prioritize the most impactful quality factors.

- Select the most critical metrics (no more than three initially) based on customer feedback and internal cross-functional teams as per the maturity of the enterprise.

- Ensure standard lingo, metrics, and effective communication channels exist.

- Automate data collection for reporting to ensure minimal effort from the teams.

- In parallel, onboard a group of quality-passionate practitioners who are not only reviewing data, but also help with shifting left by continuously focusing on quality-impacting factors to build awareness.

- Establish a baseline with agreement from business owners and executive sponsor.

- Have every department set an improvement target quarter over quarter and publish results to the executive team.

- Meet weekly with the steering committee to report on progress.

- Validate via proper internal audit with questions that properly focus on key quality-impacting pillars to make sure proper decisions are made to elevate quality in the organization. This requires a mindset shift.

- As success criteria for each initiative is reached, play into the motivational level at each maturity stage to be able to successfully continue the quality journey.

- Allow six to nine months after launching the initiative to validate effectiveness with customers; rinse and repeat.

Having a groomed backlog with a list of quality-impacting factors will allow for addressing higher-priority items first. Designing PoCs for such items before operationalizing them across the organization allows for assessing the effectiveness of the new process at a smaller scale, learning from the experience, and implementing it with much higher confidence at a larger scale. It will also allow for validating that the new process will accomplish the goal. Then, make any adjustments needed and repeat the process. That is how you can make continuous improvement!

And remember that by using the same old thinking, you can expect the same old results.

As may have already come across strongly, I am a quality-passionate individual who takes pride in helping organizations see their value and enjoy measurable positive quality improvements. In this book, I have tried to provide guidance to help steer your Agile quality transformation at all levels. This book can now become a great reference as you continuously improve and incrementally make positive changes to establish a culture of quality in your product team, business unit, and enterprise. If the concepts I have shared in this book resonate with you and you are able to see results by following certain guidelines, I would love to hear from you.

Wishing you all a successful journey!

Index

© CA 2019

N. Nader-Rezvani, *An Executive's Guide to Software Quality in an Agile Organization*,
https://doi.org/10.1007/978-1-4842-3751-9